JANE HOGAN

Pain-Free
on
PURPOSE

USE YOUR MIND TO HEAL YOUR BODY AND GET YOUR LIFE BACK

I0458747

Foreword by Dr. Aimie Apigian, MD

ISBN: 978-1-968061-27-2

Praise for *Pain-Free on Purpose*

"*Pain-Free on Purpose* is a powerful and compassionate guide for anyone struggling with chronic pain. Blending personal experience, neuroscience, and functional medicine, Jane Hogan offers a practical roadmap to healing that empowers readers to reclaim their lives. Her DESIGN Blueprint provides clear, actionable steps to regulate the nervous system and support the body's innate ability to heal. This book is a beacon of hope for those seeking true transformation and lasting relief."

—Dr. Jill Carnahan, MD, ABIHM, IFMCP, author of *Unexpected: Finding Resilience through Functional Medicine, Science, and Faith*

"Feeling safe is the core of allowing your body to heal. In *Pain-Free on Purpose*, Jane lays out a clear pathway to achieve this and thrive. Welcome to your new life."

—David Hanscom, MD, orthopedic spine surgeon and author of *Back in Control*

"If you're struggling with chronic pain, *Pain-Free on Purpose* is an absolute must-read. It reveals the empowering truth that you possess the remarkable ability to heal yourself. With Jane Hogan as your compassionate guide, you'll embark on a transformative journey to reclaim a life that's truly worth living."

—Elaine Glass, author of *Get Quiet*

"Jane Hogan's *Pain-Free on Purpose* is a powerful testament to the profound healing potential that lies within each of us. As a physician dedicated to the intersection of functional, integrative, and environmental health, I deeply resonate with Jane's empowering approach. This book beautifully guides readers through the journey of understanding chronic pain not merely as a physical symptom but as an invitation to transformative personal growth. Jane's compassionate and actionable insights offer not only relief but also a renewed sense of agency and hope. Anyone seeking to reclaim their vitality and move beyond pain into purpose-driven wellness will find immense value and inspiration in these pages. I wholeheartedly recommend *Pain-Free on Purpose* to both patients and colleagues as a transformative resource on the path to authentic healing."

—Kelly K. McCann, MD, MPH&TM,
founder and director of The Spring Center in Costa Mesa, CA

"With a beautiful balance of research and wisdom, *Pain-Free on Purpose* brings the latest in neuroscience and functional medicine to life in an accessible, empowering, and LIGHT way."

—Heather Aardema, founder of School of Living Lighter,
NBC-HWC, FMCHC, CLC, CDC

"*Pain-Free on Purpose* is the guidebook we've been waiting for—compassionate, clear, and rooted in real healing. Jane Hogan shows us how to become the hero of our own health journey. As a functional health coach dedicated to empowering people to reclaim their health through sustainable, root-cause healing, I deeply resonate with Jane's message. Her approach beautifully aligns with my own philosophy: true healing happens when we reconnect with our body's innate wisdom and take ownership of our well-being."

—Anu Simh, NBC-HWC, founder of 9 Arms of Wellness,
author of *Flourish From Within*

"*Pain-Free on Purpose* is more than a book—it's a healing companion. Jane Hogan writes with the rare kind of clarity and compassion that helps you exhale. She doesn't just offer tools—she helps you remember your body's wisdom and your own capacity to heal. Rooted in neuroscience, trauma-informed insight, and lived experience, this book gently guides you back to regulation, connection, and possibility. If you've been stuck in pain and are ready to move forward with tenderness and trust, start here."

—Michael Roesslein, MSc, FDN-P,
founder of Rebel Health & Anima Somatic Self-Discovery

"Jane Hogan has created a strong blend and balance of science and soul. *Pain-Free on Purpose* is a must-read for anyone who feels lost and in pain. When it feels like nothing is going to work, and you need hope and inspiration along with an action plan for results. Here it is."

—Shivan Sarna, founder of Chronic Condition Rescue

"If you are sick and tired of living with pain, Jane Hogan's latest book will bring you not only a sense of hope and new possibilities, but a practical, proven pathway, a safe, sustainable design for living pain-free. Born from her own personal pain journey, Jane skillfully guides you back home to your natural, comfortable, authentic self."

—Debora Wayne, founder & CEO of International Chronic Pain Institute®

"*Pain-Free on Purpose* is a compassionate, empowering invitation to reconnect with the body's innate ability to heal. As the Wellness Engineer, Jane Hogan brings a unique point of view, weaving science and spirit together in a way that nourishes not just the nervous system, but your whole self. With her gentle wisdom and with a focus on grounded research, this book offers a healing path paved with love, presence, and possibility. It's a must-read for anyone ready to reclaim their state of well-being."

—Mira Dessy, The Ingredient Guru, author of *The Pantry Principle*

"Few things are more powerful than someone transforming their own pain into purpose. In *Pain-Free on Purpose*, Jane Hogan does exactly that—offering a message of hope, grounded in science and delivered straight from the heart. If you've been living with chronic pain, this book is the blueprint you've been waiting for—one that inspires healing on every level: mind, body, and soul."

—Joe Rignola, founder of WellConnected.tv

"Jane transforms complex healing science into simple, actionable steps that actually work—because she's lived it. This book is the missing manual for anyone ready to become the architect of their own healing journey."

—Jana Danielson, founder & CEO, Bloom Better,
and author of *The Sacred Woman's Guide to Blooming Better*

"As a fellow author and health practitioner deeply committed to uncovering root causes of chronic illness, I found *Pain-Free on Purpose* to be a profoundly resonant and empowering guide. Jane Hogan has masterfully woven together scientific insight, lived experience, and heart-centered wisdom to illuminate a path toward healing that is both accessible and inspiring.

What sets this book apart is Jane's rare ability to bridge the gap between the analytical and the intuitive, between functional medicine and emotional healing. Her DESIGN Blueprint is not just a clever acronym—it's a compassionate and comprehensive system that invites readers to reclaim agency in their own health journey. From the engineering precision she brings to her investigation of pain to the soulful invitation to explore desire, surrender, and play, Jane speaks to both the skeptic and the seeker.

I was particularly moved by the honesty and vulnerability in her storytelling. Rather than positioning herself as an infallible expert, she walks alongside the reader, openly sharing the missteps and insights that shaped her evolution from engineer to wellness guide. This humility, paired with scientific rigor, makes her voice one of deep integrity and trustworthiness.

For anyone living with chronic pain—or anyone supporting those who do—*Pain-Free on Purpose* is a beacon of hope and a toolkit for transformation. Jane reminds us that healing is not just possible—it's purposeful, powerful, and within reach.

With gratitude for this essential contribution to the field."

—Dr. Keesha Ewers, PhD, ARNP, FMP-C,
author of *Solving the Autoimmune Puzzle,*
founder of the Reverse Autoimmune Disease Institute,
Functional Medicine Practitioner, Ayurvedic Health Counselor,
Trauma-Informed Healer

"*Pain-Free on Purpose* is more than a book—it's a lifeline for anyone trapped in chronic pain. Jane Hogan speaks directly to the heart of healing, blending science, spirit, and soul into a message of true empowerment. As someone who has helped countless individuals find freedom from pain through natural methods, I recognize the rare brilliance in Jane's work. This book doesn't just inform—it transforms. If you're ready to reclaim your health from the inside out, this is where your journey begins."

—Dr. Rob Vanbergen, DNM, PhD, Pain Free For Life

Medical Disclaimer

This publication contains the opinions and ideas of its author. It is intended to provide helpful and informative material on the subjects addressed in the publication. It is sold with the understanding that the author and publisher are not engaged in providing medical, health, or any other kind of professional services. The reader should consult their medical, health, or other competent professional before adopting any of the suggestions in this book or drawing references from it.

The author and publisher specifically disclaim all responsibility for any liability, loss, or risk, personal or otherwise, that is incurred as a consequence, directly or indirectly, of the use or application of any of the contents of this book.

For my family, my biggest supporters. Noel, Nick, Kelsey, and Riley.

May we all live on purpose and fulfill our destiny.

Table of Contents

FOREWORD

As a physician trained in both preventive and addiction medicine, I've stood at the intersection of chronic pain and healing. What becomes strikingly apparent from this vantage point is just how fragmented our medical approach to pain has become. We've become stuck in a system that divides the human experience and disease into discrete parts—treating the body separately from the mind, the physical separately from the emotional, the present symptoms separately from past experiences.

The roots of this disjointed approach stretch back centuries, to the Cartesian split that divided mind from body in Western thought. The 17th-century separation found fertile ground in American medicine's emphasis on specialization and intervention. By the 1990s, pain was being marketed as the "fifth vital sign," pushing physicians toward pharmaceutical solutions while the understanding of pain's biological, psychological, and social dimensions remained underdeveloped. This historical momentum led to our current crisis—where we excel at targeting symptoms but struggle to address the root factors creating and sustaining chronic pain.

In the United States alone, chronic pain affects approximately 50 million adults, with 19.6 million experiencing high-impact chronic pain that limits life or work activities. The economic burden exceeds $635 billion annually in medical costs and lost productivity—more than cancer, heart disease, and diabetes combined. The opioid crisis, in part fueled by our misguided approach to pain management, claims nearly 250 lives daily and has decreased American life expectancy for the first time in generations. Even more concerning, studies show that long-term opioid use actually increases pain sensitivity in many patients, creating a destructive cycle of escalating doses and diminishing relief. Behind all these staggering numbers are real people whose lives have been devastated. What Jane describes in the opening as her lowest point is real. It's not exaggerated.

This separation became institutionalized in our medical education and practice, creating a system where my physician colleagues and I were trained to focus on observable, measurable pathology while overlooking the role of the nervous system state, past trauma, and emotional experiences in creating and sustaining pain. We have developed remarkable technologies to image and identify structural problems. Yet we've neglected to develop even the simplest approaches to understand the body's physical expression of stored emotions and negative self-beliefs.

By addressing pain chemically but not holistically, we've upended people's lives, not just by their pain, but by our antiquated, compartmentalized approaches to treating it.

When we encounter a patient with chronic pain, how often do we ask: "What's your relationship with yourself?" rather than simply "What's wrong with you?" How often do we go deeper into the stored emotions behind physical pain, seeking acknowledgment and expression? Pain is one way the body shows us the complete inner state of a person.

Let me share just one example from the countless patients I've treated over the years. I remember a patient, a successful executive with debilitating episodes of back pain that she had assumed were a result of structural issues, and she had moved the wrong way and "thrown it out." When our conversations finally turned to her life rather than just her spine, she revealed a childhood of carrying emotional burdens no child should bear. "I always had to be the strong one," she said. Her back pain began to resolve not when we finally found the right medication, but when she learned to acknowledge, feel, and move through that emotional weight and her beliefs about herself that made it hard to relax and feel secure.

Other patients would arrive in my office, often having seen multiple specialists, carrying bags of prescriptions, and having become dependent on pain medications for relief. Yet instead of relief, they still suffered with pain and now withdrawals. Their pain had been addressed as a symptom, but the root cause remained untouched.

What we now understand is that trauma doesn't just live in memory—it becomes encoded in our very biology. Chronic activation of stress responses creates dysregulation in the autonomic nervous system, leading to inflammatory cascades, altered pain perception, and compromised immune function. Healing requires us to address the conversation between the mind and body, between past and present, between emotion and physiology.

This is why I was honored to support Jane's approach laid out in this book. Both the Biology of Trauma framework and Jane's DESIGN Blueprint emerged from the same recognition. This is precisely why Jane Hogan's book *Pain-Free on Purpose* is so vitally important for our world today. Jane has created a practical framework that works, and patients need to have this hope. Her DESIGN Blueprint offers what medication alone cannot—a systematic approach to regulating the nervous system, addressing the unconscious stress responses, maintaining pain cycles, and creating the physiological conditions where healing becomes possible. Her integration of practical tools for rewiring these biological patterns represents exactly the missing piece I witnessed in conventional medicine.

We need a paradigm shift, and I envision a healthcare system that embraces these connections—one that recognizes pain as a biopsychosocial experience requiring equally multifaceted approaches. A system that empowers patients with knowledge about their own biology and provides them with practical tools to become active participants in their healing journey. Jane's work is a significant step toward that vision.

Unfortunately, the reality is that most Western medicine practitioners will not be ready to embrace the principles laid out in this book. The paradigm shift laid out in *Pain-Free on Purpose* challenges decades of established training and practice.

However, Jane's work is revolutionary, and it doesn't wait for the system to change to create the needed revolution. It gives patients the tools they need to address the actual root causes of pain through holistic, scientifically sound principles. Jane has shown us it is possible, and this book puts the power of healing directly into the hands of those who need it most.

For anyone struggling with chronic pain, this book offers something that conventional medicine cannot right now: hope grounded in practical action. The stories, strategies, and insights Jane shares have the power to change lives—not by numbing pain temporarily, but by addressing its roots and creating the conditions for authentic healing. I am proud to be creating the paradigm shift with Jane Hogan.

If you're holding this book and living with pain, know that your experience is valid, your healing is possible, and you have found a resource in Jane who has walked this path herself and can show you the way forward.

Dr. Aimie Apigian, MD, MS, MPH
Preventive, Public Health, and Addiction Medicine Physician
Author of *The Biology of Trauma: How the Body Holds Fear, Pain, and Overwhelm, and How to Heal It*

INTRODUCTION

I lay in bed, curled up in pain, overwhelmed by despair, and wondered, *How has my life come to this?*

Just three months earlier, in February of 2016, I had celebrated my fiftieth birthday, a strong and vibrant woman, full of hope and excitement for the "freedom years" ahead. My husband and I were newly empty nesters, and retirement was just a few years away. For decades, we had dreamed of traveling the world and embracing a life free from the daily grind.

Little did I know that pain, like an uninvited guest, would soon become a constant companion, robbing me of the future I had envisioned. It crept into my joints, leaving me walking with a shuffle, as though I had aged overnight. My once-strong hands lost their grip, and my nights were spent in sleepless agony, frustration, and exhaustion.

That morning, alone in my bedroom after my husband left for work, I reached my lowest point. The pain was unbearable, but even worse was the sinking feeling that this was my new reality. I thought, *If this is how my life is going to be, I'm ready to be done.* I felt like my body had betrayed me, like I was letting down everyone I loved. I was letting myself down. The burden of my pain was too heavy to bear. How could we enjoy our freedom years if I could barely walk?

Then, in the darkness of that moment, something unexpected happened.

A whisper from inside reached out to me, a voice that felt like a loving embrace. It wasn't my voice, yet it came from within me. Whether it was my soul, an angel, or a higher power, I don't know. What I do know is that it assured me:

"This is not how your life will unfold. You will figure this out, and you will teach others."

I was still in pain, but as I wiped away my tears, something inside me shifted. A spark of hope was born. I knew I would find answers, and beyond that, I would share them with others. That moment ignited a transformational journey, one that changed the course of my life.

I'll share more about how I eventually became pain-free as we journey through this book. But for now, I want you to know this: I figured it out. And I want to help you figure it out, too.

Along my path back to wellness, I immersed myself in studying chronic pain. I love research. As an engineer, I'm wired to solve problems. I applied my mind and analytical skills to my healing journey, meticulously tracking and testing different approaches.

I explored everything: functional medicine, mind-body medicine, alternative therapies, and more. I spent thousands of dollars on naturopaths, functional medicine doctors, lab tests, and supplements. Eventually, my quest for understanding led me to become a Functional Medicine Certified Health Coach, and in 2020, after a 30-year engineering career, I left my hard hat behind to pursue my true passion: helping others break free from chronic pain.

Since then, I've read hundreds of books and scientific papers, interviewed hundreds of world-renowned experts on my Wellness by Design podcast, and hosted two online summits, Becoming Pain-Free. And I've helped thousands of people release pain in my coaching, Calm by DESIGN program, Living Pain-Free membership, You Can Heal self-study course and other programs.

I became pain-free on purpose.

I love that the word purpose is both a noun and a verb. As a noun, it means an aim or destination, reflecting one of the core messages of this book: to envision what you truly desire for your life as the pain-free version of you. As a verb, to purpose means to act with intention. Healing doesn't just happen, we create it through small, meaningful steps. My hope is that as you move through these pages, you'll embrace both meanings: crafting a clear, soul-aligned vision for your healing, and taking inspired action to bring it to life.

Pain-Free on Purpose is for anyone living with chronic pain who feels called to a deeper kind of healing, one that honors the connection between the mind, body, and spirit. It's for those who are open to the possibility that pain carries a message, and that true healing begins when we listen with compassion and courage. It's for the seekers, the soul-led, and the curious, for those who are ready to step into their own power and co-create a new reality of wellness, with science and inner wisdom working hand in hand.

This book may not be for you if you're looking for a quick fix or aren't yet willing to explore new ways of thinking, feeling, and being. Healing isn't about blame—it's about awakening. You didn't choose your pain, but you can choose your path forward.

I am not a doctor, and this book is not intended to diagnose, treat, or cure any medical condition. Instead, it provides education, guidance, and tools to support your body's innate ability to heal. While I'm here to guide you and cheer you on, you should always consult your healthcare provider before making any changes to your health routine.

Pain-Free on Purpose is built on the DESIGN Blueprint—a transformative framework that emerged through my own healing journey and from supporting thousands of others in my coaching programs. The word DESIGN is an acronym for the six key steps in the Blueprint: Desire, Explore, Surrender, Integrate, Generate, and Navigate. Each step incorporates two Healing Habits to support regulation of your nervous system. Rooted in both science and soul, this path helps calm the nervous system and awaken the body's innate ability to heal.

The book is presented in three parts. Part I: Foundations is about the science behind why your mind can be used to heal the body and why nervous system regulation is where you must begin. Part II: The DESIGN Blueprint is where I lay out the step-by-step plan and twelve simple Healing Habits to support nervous system regulation. In Part III: Life by DESIGN, I share my four-step weekly system to follow the DESIGN Blueprint to empower you throughout your life to live as the fullest expression of yourself.

As you follow along and implement the Healing Habits of the DESIGN Blueprint, I'll guide you with proven success strategies to help you integrate these habits in daily life. Along the way, I'll share personal insights from my journey. I'll share what worked, and I'll share my mistakes so you won't have to make the same ones. This book is not just about reducing pain; it's about reclaiming energy, joy, and vitality.

Most of us are unaware of the immense power within us, the power to co-create our life experiences. When we shift from living by default to living by design, we stop reacting to life and start shaping it. By learning how to use our mind to integrate the habits that regulate the nervous system, release emotional burdens, and make intentional choices, we unlock the gateway to healing.

My hope is that as you turn these pages, you will feel inspired, empowered, and deeply supported in your healing journey. You are not broken. You are powerful beyond measure.

Let's begin.

PAIN-FREE ON PURPOSE

Use Your Mind to Heal Your Body and Get Your Life Back

PART I:
Foundations

Chapter 1

The Missing Puzzle Piece in Pain Relief

"The body keeps the score, but the mind holds the key."
—Dr. Bessel van der Kolk

A year before the onset of my pain symptoms, my mother died very suddenly. She was my best friend and biggest champion, and the grief I felt was soul-wrenching. On top of the deep sadness, I was her executor, responsible for handling her estate since my father had passed years earlier. My parents had been travelers and collectors, and after living in their home for fifty years, there was a lot to deal with. The house was an eight-hour drive away, and with three siblings, tensions inevitably surfaced as I did my best to manage everything fairly and prepare the home for sale.

I was hardly sleeping. My heart was constantly racing. I was deep in sadness. Almost a year to the day after my mother passed, the pain began.

At first, it was just my shoulder. The pain was so severe that I needed a sling for support. The next day, the other shoulder. Then, my feet and hands started to ache. Over the next several weeks, pain traveled to almost every joint in my body. My knees swelled up, my grip strength vanished, and within three months, I could barely walk. Even basic self-care became difficult.

My husband was supportive but felt helpless. Neither of us knew what to do.

And then, at my lowest moment when I was curled up in dispair, I heard that reassuring voice telling me I would figure this out. That whisper changed everything. From then on, I had hope and a deep inner knowing that healing was possible.

As an engineer, I believed that everything was figure-outable. I started tracking, testing, and analyzing my progress. I delved into anti-inflammatory diets, consulted naturopaths, and embraced lifestyle changes. The pain and inflammation started to decrease, but something was still missing. I had done everything "right," yet I was still in pain.

Then, things got worse.

I was diagnosed with rheumatoid arthritis, an autoimmune condition with no known cure. My rheumatologist recommended medications with side effects that terrified me more than the pain itself. By that point, I had seen some improvements from my lifestyle changes, so I made the personal choice to hold off on medication while I continued experimenting on myself. My doctor was supportive but had no other tools to offer.

I was on my own again. More fear crept in.

I felt like I was in a battle against time, trying to heal my body before "permanent destruction" (yes, these were the exact words I heard) of my joints set in. I had to figure this out. Fast.

Something deep inside told me that the pain was related to the extreme stress I had experienced in the year leading up to its onset. If stress had turned on the pain, I reasoned, then my body had the capacity to turn it off.

But how?

I needed to understand exactly how stress impacts the body.

Stress Is Not the Event—It's the Response

For years, I had believed stress was something external, like a demanding job, a difficult relationship, or a major life event. But during an interview with Dr. Aimie Apigian for my Becoming Pain-Free summit, I learned something that changed my perspective completely.

She explained that stress isn't the event itself. Stress is the body's *response* to the event.

That made so much sense.

Two people can experience the exact same situation, yet one may be overwhelmed while the other is unbothered. Why? Because our nervous systems interpret and process stress differently, shaped by our past experiences, subconscious programming, and unresolved emotions.

Years before my pain began, I had borrowed a book from the library by Louise Hay, *You Can Heal Your Life*. I remember being fascinated by the concepts Hay shared in that book, that thoughts could influence physical health. With my new understanding of stress as a root cause, I revisited the book and flipped to the section on rheumatoid arthritis.

Hay's description of the thought processes linked to rheumatoid arthritis stopped me in my tracks: "Deep criticism of authority. Feeling very put upon."

I felt those words in my bones.

The weight of my responsibilities, the burden of trying to hold everything together, and the unspoken pressure I had carried made sense. I realized that if I truly wanted to heal, I needed to look beyond food, supplements, and lifestyle changes. I needed to address why my body had responded in the way it did to the stress I was under. And that led me to the nervous system.

How the Nervous System Works

Controlling all our bodily functions, movement, sensations, thoughts, and feelings is the central nervous system (CNS). The CNS includes the brain, with its various parts that work together, including the retina of the eyes, and the spinal cord, the bundle of nerves that are responsible for transmitting messages between the brain and the body.

Receiving input from the CNS is the autonomic nervous system (ANS), which regulates involuntary regulatory processes in the body. Organs falling under the control of the ANS include the skin, heart and circulatory system, immune system, lungs, intestines, colon, liver, pancreas, urinary tract, and reproductive system.

There are two modes of operation of the ANS: the parasympathetic state and the sympathetic state. The parasympathetic state is what should be the "business as usual" mode of the ANS. This is the state where the body is in "rest and digest" mode. The sympathetic state is activated to help the body in times of stress or danger, to help us deal with an immediate crisis through the "fight or flight" mode. When in the parasympathetic state, we are experiencing the relaxation response of the nervous system. In the sympathetic state, we are in the stress response.

When all is well, in the relaxation response of the nervous system, the body performs all its regular functions fabulously. When triggered by stress, the ANS springs into action like an emergency first responder and switches to the stress response. Under the stress response, many regular body functions are suspended as the body prepares to fight, flee, or freeze. Heart rate increases, adrenaline is released, the bladder relaxes, blood is directed to the major muscle groups, pupils dilate, airways dilate, saliva production is inhibited, and cognitive thinking slows down.

We are built to handle short-term stress. The stress response of the nervous system is a good thing. It's there to protect us in life-threatening situations, so we have the strength to fight or flee or do what we need to do to protect ourselves.

The problem is that our everyday modern lives are filled with experiences that are interpreted by the CNS as life-threatening. Your boss expressing dissatisfaction with your work, an upcoming presentation, or an email from the tax agency, all are interpreted as threats. As the saying goes, our brains can't tell the difference between taxes and tigers; both are equally dangerous as far as our nervous system is concerned. When stress is too much or becomes chronic, the ANS gets "stuck" in the stress response, or a state of *nervous system dysregulation*.

The Mind Creates the Body

I remember hearing spiritual leader, author, and alternative health advocate Deepak Chopra say, "The mind creates the body." Initially, I thought he meant this figuratively, not literally. But as I studied and learned more, I realized that the mind does, literally, create the body by way of the nervous system, the master controller.

A pioneer in the study of how the body responds to the mind was Candace Pert, a neuroscientist and pharmacologist. Her research showed that the brain produces neuropeptides, proteins that act as neurotransmitters and hormones, in response to emotions. She found that neuropeptides play a critical role in regulating the body's response to stress, highlighting the impact of emotions on physiological states. Pert's research proved that there is a biochemical link between the mind and the body, published in her groundbreaking book, *Molecules of Emotion: The Science Behind Mind-Body Medicine*. She showed that emotions such as anger, grief, fear, and joy are not simply psychological states but have a direct impact on the physiological processes in the body. Pert believed that the body has an innate intelligence regulating its functions and enabling healing, and it is *emotions* that can help or hinder healing (Pert, 1997).

Let's go a little deeper into the interaction between thoughts and emotions by considering the response of our cells. Each cell in our body has thousands of receptors, and each receptor is specifically matched to one peptide, or protein. Every thought we have, such as happiness, sadness, anger, irritation, guilt, joy, and so on, releases a flurry of neuropeptides associated with that thought. Those neuropeptides travel through the body and connect with the matching receptors on the surface of each cell. The cell responds by changing its function and structure to meet the needs of the neuropeptides it receives. As the cell divides, the new cell that is produced through its division will have more receptors to match the neuropeptides it is more often exposed to, and fewer receptors for neuropeptides that its mother cell was not exposed to as frequently. Therefore, if you have been bombarding your cells with neuropeptides from negative thoughts, your cells are reproducing to receive more of those neuropeptides in the future, and there will be fewer receptors for positive thought neuropeptides. In the long term, this will make you inclined towards negativity. If you've been inclined toward negative thinking, don't lose heart, because our cells are in constant turnover, and over time, we can use our thoughts to create more receptors for neuropeptides associated with positive thoughts. By so doing, we will be making cells that shift the entire body toward health and well-being.

How the immune system responds to emotions is a newer area of scientific research gaining attention, called psychoneuroimmunology (PNI). This field of science examines how the mind, nervous system, and immune system work together in the body. Research in this area has shown that our thoughts and emotions can impact the body's immune response. When the immune system is triggered, the result is inflammation. Chronic stressful emotions can lead to chronic inflammation anywhere in the body, and with inflammation comes pain. The study of PNI has shown that positive emotions, such as gratitude, joy, and love, impact the immune system in a positive way, which can reduce inflammation and improve a variety of health markers, while negative emotions have the opposite effect.

In *The Biology of Belief: Unleashing the Power of Consciousness, Matter, and Miracles*, cell biologist Dr. Bruce Lipton dives deep into this revolutionary understanding of human biology and how genes respond to our thoughts and emotions. For decades, the dominant narrative in science was that we are the sum of our genes, locked into whatever genetic hand we've been dealt. However, Lipton and other pioneering researchers showed that DNA isn't the master switch we thought it was. Instead, our genes take their cues from signals outside the cell. This discovery birthed a groundbreaking field of science known as epigenetics, which literally means "above the genes" (Lipton, 2005).

Through the lens of epigenetics, we now understand that genes can switch on or off in response to environmental signals. It's not the genes themselves dictating outcomes; it's the environment they're exposed to that drives their expression. Stress and emotions play pivotal roles in how our genes express themselves, influencing everything from cellular repair to immune function. Imagine your genes as dimmer switches, adjusting their intensity based on the messages they receive. In this light, we have significant influence over gene expression with our thoughts and feelings. This means your genes are not your destiny. They're just part of the story, and you hold the pen to write your own new story, one without pain.

Behaviors of Protection

As I delved deeper into my research, I discovered that there are clues revealing nervous system dysregulation, long before chronic pain shows up. One way we can gain insight into the state of the nervous system is to observe our behaviors.

Many of our daily habitual behaviors began early in life. As Gabor Maté explains in *When the Body Says No*, we form "behavioral adaptations" as a form of protection (Maté, 2003). When we are little, we can't "fight" or "flee," so we develop behaviors to protect ourselves instead, to cope with an underlying sense of stress or threat.

When the nervous system is stuck in a chronic state of fight, flight, or freeze, protective behavioral adaptations often emerge. These can include:

- **People-pleasing**: Prioritizing others' needs to avoid conflict.
- **Perfectionism**: Striving for impossible standards to feel in control.
- **Over-politeness**: Avoiding disagreement, even at the expense of self-expression.
- **Hypervigilance**: Constantly reading others' moods for signs of danger.
- **Trouble setting boundaries**: Feeling guilty for saying no.
- **Sensitivity to criticism**: Taking feedback personally, even when well-intended.
- **Neglecting self-care**: Putting others before yourself.
- **Hyper-independence**: Believing "I have to do everything on my own."

Do you recognize yourself in many of these patterns? Whenever I speak to groups of people with chronic pain and ask them if they identify with any of these behaviors, I often hear people say, "All of them." I see these behaviour adaptations in so many of my clients and students too. Why do so many of us develop these patterns? Because they once served a purpose. They helped us stay safe, gain acceptance, or avoid painful experiences. The problem is, when these adaptations become deeply ingrained, they keep the nervous system in a constant state of stress and then begin to show up in the body as physical symptoms.

I also had these behavioral adaptations. I had a lifetime of people-pleasing and perfectionism. Even though I was a "good girl" and became an engineer like my father wanted me to, I never felt smart enough or that I was doing what I really wanted. I was a busy working mother, yet I still ran the chess club at the kids' school, was president of the swim club, swim meet manager whenever we hosted swimming competitions, and on and on. I was trying to do it all, and I did a good job, yet I never felt good enough. Over time, and by following the strategies I'll share with you in this book, I fall back into these patterns less frequently. When I let go of these protective thoughts and behaviors, my body can let go of pain, too.

From Protective Behaviors to Protection in the Body

While behaviors can reveal that the nervous system is in protection mode, so can the language of the body. First, there may be whispers: muscle tension, bracing, tightness, restless sleep, digestive issues, or skin irritations. Then, the whispers turn into shouts like persistent pain, chronic inflammation, autoimmune conditions, migraines, or irritable bowel issues.

Chronic pain is the brain's way of protecting us because it perceives, based on signals from the nervous system, that we are in danger. When you go back in time, can you see a connection between your prevailing emotions that may have led to physical pain or illness? You could have had some underlying or hidden chronic stress, and then a big stress event that became too much. Or it could be low-grade stress that's always there? Perhaps your internal dialogue about yourself and the world around you is predominantly negative. At some point, the brain will begin to let you know that "enough is enough" and turn on protection in the form of chronic pain.

Nervous system dysregulation as a root cause doesn't just apply to rheumatoid arthritis. Most chronic pain and, to a large extent, most chronic health conditions, are related to stress. A 2013 article in the *Journal of the American Medical Association (JAMA)* indicated that

60% to 80% of primary care physician visits may have a stress-related component (Nerurkar et al., 2013). Yet, most primary care does not address stress as a root cause, and focuses instead on treating the symptoms of stress, whether that's mystery symptoms, illness, or pain. This prolonged state of alert affects other body systems, such as the digestive, immune, and hormonal systems, leading to downstream effects like digestive issues, skin rashes, difficulty sleeping, fatigue, disease, and chronic pain.

For the body to function optimally and heal, the nervous system must be addressed. By shifting the nervous system back to the parasympathetic state and being able to regulate itself, the body is better able to do its healing work naturally … and release pain.

Putting the Puzzle Pieces Together

In my engineering days, I had to design structures that could withstand expected stresses during service life. Codes and standards have built-in factors of safety so that the supporting structures should never have to carry loads that would exceed the stress the materials can carry. If the structure is overloaded, the stress becomes too much and the structure fails, sometimes with warning signs first, and sometimes the failure is sudden and catastrophic. This can happen with people, too. When the stress becomes too much, beyond our capacity, our "structure" can begin to fail.

Now that we have found the missing puzzle piece in chronic pain treatment, we can see the whole picture. The first area to address is the nervous system. When we get the nervous system regulated, all other systems begin to work more effectively. Eventually, once it feels "safe," the brain can release its need for protection, tell the nervous system to relax, and the body can heal and let go of pain.

In my own journey, although I knew my year of extreme stress had been the trigger that turned on pain in my body, I had been focusing on the wrong things. I had been following anti-inflammatory diets to the point where I developed orthorexia, a fear of eating anything but "healthy" food. My extreme focus on my health had left me socially isolated. I stopped finding joy in life because I had been putting so much pressure on myself to heal. Instead, the one thing I needed to focus on was regulating my nervous system.

Let's get you started on nervous system regulation with two exercises. I like to call these "Heartwork"—not homework!

Heartwork

1. Create Your Healing Sanctuary

Learning to regulate your nervous system will take time and dedication, and ideally, you have a safe place to do this work, which I call the healing sanctuary. Your healing sanctuary is a designated space in your home where you can have privacy and not be disturbed. It could be a separate room in your home or a corner of a room. There should be comfortable seating, good lighting, which you can turn off easily, and a blanket in case you get chilled. You want this space to feel sacred, like your own personal temple. Have photographs of people you love and people who love you. Include mementos from places that are special to you, crystals or other special objects, words that inspire you, or whatever trinkets are especially meaningful to you. This is your special place. Let it inspire you and let it grow and change with you. Once you have created your healing sanctuary, notice how you feel when you sit down in this space. Do you feel more at peace when you are in your healing sanctuary? I hope so.

2. Journaling for Insights: The Missing Link for Healing

The journey to healing begins with awareness. If the nervous system has been in a chronic stress response, it is often trying to protect us from something, whether it's an old fear, a deep emotional wound, or an unconscious belief. One of the most powerful ways to access these insights is through journaling.

Take a moment to reflect and write:

1. **How is pain trying to protect me?**
   Consider whether your pain might be a signal from your body, trying to keep you safe from something, like overwork, emotional pain, or unspoken fears.
2. **What stress or emotional burdens was I carrying in the months leading up to my pain?**
   Look for patterns between your life experiences and your symptoms.
3. **What am I holding onto, physically, emotionally, or mentally, that I need to release?**
   The body holds onto emotions and stress. Sometimes, healing starts with recognizing what needs to be let go.

Write without judgment. Let the words flow. You may be surprised at what emerges.

Key Chapter Takeaways

- Stress goes hand-in-hand with chronic pain.
- Stress is not an event; it is a response of the nervous system.
- Chronic activation of the sympathetic response of the nervous system causes nervous system dysregulation.
- Nervous system dysregulation shows up as behavioral adaptations and "protection" in the body.
- Every cell in the body is in a constant state of regeneration in response to thoughts and feelings.
- The missing puzzle piece in pain treatment is not addressing the true root cause of most chronic pain conditions: nervous system dysregulation.

Chapter 2

The Biggest Mistake People Make That Reinforces Pain

*"We cannot solve our problems with the same thinking
we used when we created them."*
—Albert Einstein

Once I discovered the connection between stress and pain, it was clear that my body had turned on pain to protect me because my nervous system was in a state of dysregulation. It seemed obvious that if I could solve this one thing, my body could let go of the pain. I knew that my mother's passing and the aftermath of being the executor had been incredibly stressful, and that had certainly brought on the pain initially. Although I continued to miss my mother, two years later, I was no longer in deep grief. I had also completed my executor duties, so the stress associated with that role had ended. Still, I was in pain. Why was my body still feeling the need to protect me?

Deep down, I knew there was a life force in me, in us all, that wanted to heal. This wisdom of the body turns on natural self-repair mechanisms for healing. We get a cut, and our body swings into action, doing what it needs to do to seal up the wound, prevent infection, and create new tissue to heal the damage.

I reflected on high school biology lessons where we learned that the body is in a constant state of renewal, repairing and replacing old cells. Of the thirty trillion cells in the human body, about 330 billion cells are replaced *every day* (Fischetti & Christiansen, 2021). Some cells renew more quickly than others. For example, the cells that line the stomach are replaced every two days, while bone cells regenerate about every ten years (Landeros, 2024). Why, then, does the body sometimes not repair? What prevents the body from turning on its natural self-healing in every situation? Why do some people have illnesses or pains that last for years and years?

For people with chronic pain, although the body is renewing, there's a mechanism interfering with *healthy* renewal. Instead, the body is getting messages to renew in a faulty way, a *protective* way.

Somehow, even though the external stress in my life had ended, my body was still getting a faulty message and still sensed danger. We already know from the previous chapter that the nervous system is responsible for sending those signals to the body. To understand why the nervous system was continuing to "protect" me, I needed to look at the driver of the nervous system: thoughts and beliefs.

The Brain, the Mind, and Your Thoughts

We often use the words brain, mind, and thoughts interchangeably. Yet, these three are distinct and play different roles in shaping how we perceive the world and, ultimately, how we heal. Understanding their differences is crucial for reclaiming your body's ability to regulate pain and restore balance.

The brain is the physical organ inside the skull, composed of billions of neurons communicating through electrical and chemical signals. It governs bodily functions, processes sensory input, and acts as the command center for movement, reflexes, and automatic functions like breathing and digestion. It's the hardware of the body's operating system, stunningly complex but ultimately neutral. What determines how the brain functions is what runs through it: the mind.

The mind is not a physical structure but rather the realm of consciousness, where thoughts, beliefs, emotions, and interpretations arise. Think of the mind like the software that programs how the brain processes information. While the brain can be measured and scanned, the mind remains intangible, yet its effects are very real.

The mind operates on two levels: the conscious and the subconscious. Your conscious mind is the part of you that is aware of your thoughts in the present moment. It's what you use to focus, make choices, and direct attention. You can intentionally decide to take a deep breath, notice your pain, or think about what you want for lunch.

But your subconscious mind is where most thoughts occur. It's a vast, powerful database storing every experience, belief, and learned behavior you've accumulated throughout life. This matters for pain because much of what you feel is not just about physical signals from your body; it's about how your subconscious mind interprets those signals based on past experiences, emotional associations, and deeply ingrained beliefs.

Thoughts are the mental impulses that arise from both the conscious and subconscious mind. They trigger chemical and physiological responses in the body, shaping how the nervous system operates. Fear-based or stressful thoughts, whether conscious or subconscious, activate the sympathetic nervous system, sending the body into a fight-or-flight state. This increases tension, inflammation, and pain sensitivity. Calm, supportive, and positive thoughts engage the parasympathetic nervous system, which promotes relaxation, repair, and healing.

Understanding the Subconscious Mind

The subconscious mind is a storehouse of our accumulated information and experiences. Like a computer, it holds our memories, emotions, beliefs, and perceptions. A key feature of the subconscious mind is its ability to process and store vast amounts of information. The subconscious mind runs the body and our day-to-day habits, and its role is to protect us from real or perceived danger. Like a computer with programs and apps, the subconscious mind simply responds to inputs, and the installed programs respond with an output according to the quality of the programs. If the programs have "glitches", the output reflects those "glitches".

A primary function of the subconscious mind is its role in the formation and execution of habits and automatic behaviors. Habits are formed through conscious repetition and reinforcement. Once learned, the subconscious mind takes over running habits to free up the conscious mind for creative thinking. When I interviewed Dr. Bruce Lipton for my 2022 Becoming Pain-Free summit, he said 95% of our behaviors are running on autopilot from programs stored in our subconscious mind, which means that only 5% are conscious behaviors.

Think about when you were a child learning to ride a bicycle. That required concentration and focus, but once you learned how to ride, that program got stored in your subconscious mind. Now you don't have to consciously think about it, you just get on the bike and off you go.

The subconscious mind also plays a role in our emotional responses. It is connected to the limbic system, the part of the brain responsible for emotions and memory. Through conditioning, the subconscious mind associates an emotion with certain stimuli or experiences. The stronger the emotion, the more powerful the response. For example, if we had an experience of feeling extremely embarrassed when we were laughed at in front of a group of people, then we may feel fear or anxiety when we encounter a similar experience, even if we can't remember specific details of the past event. In our subconscious mind, not being accepted by our "tribe" means danger, so any situation that our subconscious mind perceives as dangerous evokes a fear response.

If your subconscious mind is filled with unprocessed emotional memories, self-doubt, or deep-seated fears, it will continue triggering the nervous system into stress and inflammation, even when there's no actual physical danger.

Beliefs Shape Your Reality

If thoughts have the power to influence the nervous system and shape how we experience pain, what happens when those thoughts become deeply ingrained patterns? These become our beliefs. Beliefs are not just fleeting thoughts; they are deeply embedded mental programs that act as filters through which we perceive the world, our bodies, and our ability to heal. They operate primarily in the subconscious mind, influencing our emotions, decisions, and even our biology—often without us realizing it.

Some beliefs empower healing, while others can keep us stuck in patterns of pain and limitation. But where do these beliefs come from? How do they get wired into our subconscious? And, most importantly, can they be changed?

Science shows us that beliefs can be powerful enough to shape our physical reality. The placebo effect, where belief in healing triggers actual physiological improvements, is one of the most well-documented demonstrations of the mind-body connection. Imagine experiencing real, measurable relief from symptoms, or even developing side effects, without having taken any active medication. This isn't just a quirk of science; it's a testament to the incredible power of the human mind.

Consider the fascinating results of placebo surgeries. In some controlled studies, people undergoing procedures, like knee surgery, were divided into two groups. One group received the full surgical intervention, while the placebo group had only an incision made before being stitched up without any corrective procedure performed. Astonishingly, many in the placebo group reported significant improvement in their symptoms simply because they believed they had undergone real surgery

(Wartolowska et al., 2014). It wasn't the scalpel that healed them; it was their belief in the healing.

Phantom limb pain offers another compelling example of the power of the mind. Individuals who have lost a limb often report feeling intense sensations, such as itching, pressure, or even excruciating pain, in the missing limb. The limb is gone, yet the pain is real (Ramachandran & Hirstein, 1998). It's not imagined suffering; it's tangible, rooted in the brain's neural pathways, which continue to signal pain from a body part that no longer exists. The mind holds onto the memory, and the body listens.

Consider also the phenomenon of delayed pain experienced by backcountry hikers or soldiers in battle who suffer a severe injury while alone. Despite the trauma, they feel no pain as they make their arduous journey to safety. Their brain, prioritizing survival, suppresses the pain response to allow them to focus on escaping danger. Only once they reach help does the pain emerge, sometimes intensely (Beecher, 1955). The brain, having fulfilled its duty to ensure survival, now switches gears to protect the body through immobilization and healing.

The power of the mind to influence the body is even more incredible when you consider documented cases of people with dissociative identity disorder (formerly known as multiple personality disorder). These reveal that one personality within the same body can exhibit clinical signs of an illness, such as diabetes, confirmed through blood tests, while another personality has no trace of the condition (Putnam, 1989). There have even been reports of different eye colors between personalities. How is this possible? It's the profound influence of the mind's perception on the body's physiology. Our thoughts don't just influence us, they shape us.

What ties all these examples together? The brain. It's the gatekeeper of our sensory experiences, including pain. Pain isn't just a signal of damage; it's a protective mechanism, activated when the brain perceives a threat. But that perception isn't always accurate. The brain can become overprotective, like an anxious parent.

Understanding the power of the mind and its influence on the brain and our biology isn't just an academic exercise. It's a profound reminder that our thoughts, beliefs, and perceptions can shape our physical reality. The programs installed in our subconscious mind influence our beliefs and our perception of reality. A belief is the acceptance of an idea by the mind that something is true, whether or not it is actually true. We form beliefs through our past experiences, the influence of people in our lives, cultural influences, and our own perceptions of events. Beliefs are thoughts we think over and over as we perceive the world around us until they become installed in our subconscious mind. These subconscious beliefs form the lens through which the conscious mind operates, influencing our thoughts and behaviors in ways we may not be aware of.

The next logical question is, how do we shape our beliefs so that they support healing and release pain? Let's first consider where our beliefs come from.

The Child Inside: The Foundation of Beliefs

The child we once were gave birth to the adult we are now. All our experiences have formed the thoughts, beliefs, and behaviors we now have. In a sense, we inherited our present from our past.

Before the age of seven, the developing brain is extremely suggestible. Research of brain activity in young children has shown that up to about age six, children are in a brain state similar to a hypnotic trance. In this suggestible state, children form many beliefs about themselves and the world. Some of these beliefs may be based on facts, and others may be based on the child's perceptions of events. Since the child's analytical mind hasn't been developed, the subconscious mind may be—and often is—programmed with information that simply isn't true. Unless we consciously change the programs that have been installed in our subconscious mind, those programs are running our lives, affecting our behaviors and biology.

Early childhood experiences that occur while the brain is still developing can be particularly impactful, with long-term repercussions on physical and mental health. Beginning in 1995, the Adverse Childhood Experiences (ACE) Study surveyed over 17,000 adults regarding their exposure to ten categories of adverse childhood experiences and their current health habits and status (Petruccelli et al., 2019). Categories included physical, emotional, and sexual abuse, neglect, household dysfunction, and divorce. The study found that the more adverse events experienced in childhood, the more likely the adult was to have chronic disease, mental issues, and social problems. The study also found that adverse childhood experiences were common, with nearly two-thirds of study participants experiencing at least one adverse event. As a result of the compelling evidence of this study, the field of trauma-informed care has grown tremendously, as well as public policies regarding early intervention for children living in adverse conditions. Many websites offer quizzes to determine your ACE score. The original score was based on ten questions, but some organizations have added more questions, expanding the range of adverse experiences. More recent studies have found that factors such as the existence of supportive relationships, healthy gestation and birth, and individual temperament have a moderating effect on negative outcomes.

The Impact of Trauma

We've all experienced trauma on some level. The effects of trauma are difficult to measure because what may be traumatic for one person may not be so for another. We tend to think of trauma as an event, but trauma, like stress, is the response of the nervous system to an event. Two people experiencing the same traumatic event may have very different responses in their nervous systems.

Most often when we think of trauma, what comes to mind are major traumatic events, often called "Big T" trauma, like mental, physical, and sexual abuse, neglect, experiencing violence, witnessing horrific events, or unexpected loss, the events that are the foundation of the original ACE score questions. However, the effects of minor, or "Little t," trauma can also be very impactful. A child who is teased, bullied, criticized, or feels lonely or unloved forms beliefs reflecting those experiences.

I hadn't experienced big trauma, but I had underestimated the impact of little trauma. From a very young age, I was relentlessly teased by one of my siblings. I cried a lot, began to stutter, and was teased for being a crybaby and stuttering. In my small child world, I didn't feel welcomed or safe to express myself. Considering these early childhood experiences, it's no surprise that I developed feelings of unworthiness, and that these lingered into adulthood. As I considered nervous system dysregulation as a root cause, I knew these childhood experiences were a contributing factor. It was clear that the behavioral adaptations I mentioned in the previous chapter were formed by my need to create safety when I was little.

In his book, *When the Body Says No: The Cost of Hidden Stress*, Gabor Maté states, "The non-complaining stoicism exhibited by rheumatoid patients is a coping style acquired early in life." A 1969 medical-psychiatric study for the Maryland Chapter of the Arthritis and Rheumatism Foundation found commonalities in psychological characteristics, vulnerabilities, and life conflicts. One behavioral characteristic common among participants with rheumatoid arthritis was described as *compensating hyper-independence*. To cope with emotional needs being ignored or not fully met, the child takes on the belief that they must meet their own emotional needs, developing a lifelong habit of pseudo-independence, and a deep reluctance to ask for help (Shochet et al., 1969).

This was me exactly. I spent a lifetime not asking for help, believing I could do it all myself and that this was an admirable quality. How wrong I was! When I began to look at my pain through this lens, everything changed. I realized that my body wasn't just breaking down for no reason. My body was responding to unresolved stress and emotional strain that had built up over my lifetime, and the final straw that broke the camel's back was the stress that came after my mother's passing. On the surface, I didn't think I had much stress in my early life, but looking deeper, I knew I had some deep issues that I had been ignoring.

Did you have experiences in your early life that may have contributed to the pain you're experiencing now? Whether you experienced "Little t" trauma or "Big T" trauma in childhood, the chronic pain you have now may well be related to stressful events you experienced as a child. To protect you, your child's mind created ways to cope with the stress to make it less overwhelming. You formed thoughts, beliefs, and behaviors as adaptations, and those became the programs in your subconscious mind. Because the subconscious mind runs the body, eventually, that stress and other life stressors revealed themselves as pain in the body.

Although it's tempting to look back at our childhood experiences and blame others for installing programs in our mind that may be contributing to our current situation, holding on to blame, resentment, anger, and similar emotions keeps the nervous system in a stressed state. We simply want to be aware of how these programs are showing up our current thought patterns and behaviors so that we can reprogram the subconscious mind with new thoughts and habits that serve our well-being. There may be some forgiveness work to do, like I did, to release feelings of blame, resentment, hurt, or anger. I'll be covering that later in Part II when we dive into the DESIGN Blueprint.

Repeating the Patterns

At this point, we've learned that the body is constantly responding and adapting to the environment in and around us, including our perceived thoughts about that environment, through a cascade of physiological and chemical pathways. Repeated thoughts, especially emotionally charged thoughts, create beliefs and programs stored in the subconscious mind. Many of these programs were formed because of childhood stress, and others were formed later in life, creating physical and behavioral adaptations to keep us "safe." Most of the time, we are operating from those subconscious beliefs in our behaviors, habitual thoughts, and habits. The subconscious mind runs the body through these thought filters.

Once you begin experiencing pain, very naturally, you'll also have fear about the pain. I remember having those fearful thoughts when I was in deep pain. I worried about the future, if I was going to be able to manage the stairs in my house, or if I could even look after myself. Sadness fell over me whenever I thought about the traveling or hiking I wouldn't be able to do. Little did I know that these emotions were perpetuating the pain because these very thoughts were triggering a stress response, which increased the pain. In other words, I was keeping myself stuck in a pain-fear cycle, which kept turning on "protection" in the form of pain.

A New Understanding

Once I saw that the pain I was experiencing was just my mind's way of protecting me, I was ready to listen. Initially, I thought that it was the stress of my mother's passing and dealing with her estate that was the root cause of the stress that led to rheumatoid arthritis. I later realized that this was simply the tipping point, the point that caused my bucket to overflow and spill. Now I could see that for most of my life, I was in a chronically stressed state, although this was so normal for me that I didn't know I was stressed. Eventually, my immune system got so confused, it began firing on my own tissues with autoimmunity. At a deep level, I was telling my body to reject itself.

The picture became clearer for me. Not only was there grief and responsibility following my mother's passing, but I had also been plagued my whole life with self-doubt, people-pleasing, perfectionism, inability to say no, and constantly worrying about what other people thought of me. These feelings were with me as long as I could remember. The mild trauma of being teased by my sibling left its mark on my emotional well-being and was reignited by tensions during my role as executor of my mother's estate. Clearly, if I wanted to help my body heal, I had to address deeper emotional issues and stop repeating patterns that were keeping my nervous system dysregulated. This included all the pressure I was putting on myself to heal. Subconscious thoughts and beliefs, along with my entire focus on "healing," were piling on the stress and not giving my body the environment it needed to heal. I was blocking my healing!

The good news is that if our repeated thoughts and behavioral patterns can contribute to pain, they can also contribute to healing. By bringing awareness to subconscious patterns, learning to regulate the nervous system, and shifting our beliefs, we can rewire our responses, calm the body, and create the internal conditions for healing.

Considering what we've learned so far, can you see that the chronic pain you are experiencing reflects your thoughts based on past conditioning? Remembering that the subconscious mind is like a computer, to change the output of chronic pain, we need to change the input.

You now understand that your past thoughts, beliefs, and behaviors are mirrored in your physical body. Since thoughts, beliefs, and behaviors can be changed, you can and will, by following the six-step plan in this book, create a new version of you that will allow the body to do its healing work naturally.

In this chapter, we've learned that the mind has a profound effect on how we live our lives and our physical bodies. Your mind's interpretation of your life experiences created the physical condition that has led to chronic pain. Obviously, you didn't make a conscious decision to create pain in your body, and my intention certainly isn't for you to "blame" yourself for the pain. What I want you to understand is that the pain in your body is evidence of how powerful your mind is and that you can use your thoughts to reprogram your subconscious mind.

Now, I ask you to reflect on your experience with chronic pain. Can you see how your mind, your thoughts, and your emotions have played a role in the onset of pain and perpetuating the pain cycle? I hope that in this chapter I have helped you see that your repeating conscious and subconscious thoughts are contributing to your health condition, and in the next chapter, we'll learn how to stop repeating those patterns.

Heartwork

1. How Your Past Shows Up in Your Present

This quiz will help you explore behavioral adaptations and tendencies based on subconscious programming, which may be linked to the chronic pain you are experiencing. Please remember that this quiz is intended for self-reflection and awareness and is not a diagnostic tool. Answer each question honestly, choosing the answer that best fits your typical behavioral patterns.

1. Do you often find it difficult to say "no" to others?

    a. Rarely or never
    b. Occasionally
    c. Frequently

d. Almost always

2. Are you highly self-critical and have difficulty accepting compliments or praise?

    a. Rarely or never
    b. Occasionally
    c. Frequently
    d. Almost always

3. Do you tend to take on responsibilities that later turn out to be more than you can easily handle?

    a. Rarely or never
    b. Occasionally
    c. Frequently
    d. Almost always

4. Do you like to be in control of situations and outcomes?

    a. Rarely or never
    b. Occasionally
    c. Frequently
    d. Almost always

5. How often are you on high alert or easily startled?

    a. Rarely or never
    b. Occasionally
    c. Frequently
    d. Almost always

6. Do you avoid expressing your needs to others?

    a. Rarely or never
    b. Occasionally

    c.   Frequently

    d.   Almost always

7. Do you criticize, judge, or gossip about other people?

    a.   Rarely or never

    b.   Occasionally

    c.   Frequently

    d.   Almost always

8. How often are you overwhelmed by feelings of resentment or anger?

    a.   Rarely or never

    b.   Occasionally

    c.   Frequently

    d.   Almost always

9. Do you rely on alcohol or other substances to help you relax?

    a.   Rarely or never

    b.   Occasionally

    c.   Frequently

    d.   Almost always

10. Do you have difficulty letting go of possessions and tend to hang on to things?

    a.   Rarely or never

    b.   Occasionally

    c.   Frequently

    d.   Almost always

11. Do you engage in binge-watching TV shows, movies, podcasts, or other media?

a. Rarely or never
b. Occasionally
c. Frequently
d. Almost always

12. Do you tend to engage in impulsive buying or excessive shopping?

    a. Rarely or never
    b. Occasionally
    c. Frequently
    d. Almost always

13. Do you withdraw from social interactions or tend to isolate yourself?

    a. Rarely or never
    b. Occasionally
    c. Frequently
    d. Almost always

14. Are you generally shy or uncomfortable in social situations?

    a. Rarely or never
    b. Occasionally
    c. Frequently
    d. Almost always

15. Are you highly sensitive to external stimuli, such as noise or bright lights?

    a. Rarely or never
    b. Occasionally
    c. Frequently
    d. Almost always

16. Do you frequently experience feelings of sadness, hopelessness, or lack of interest in activities?

    a. Rarely or never
    b. Occasionally
    c. Frequently
    d. Almost always

17. Are you critical of yourself, your body, or have low self-esteem?

    a. Rarely or never
    b. Occasionally
    c. Frequently
    d. Almost always

18. Do you have trouble maintaining healthy boundaries in relationships?

    a. Rarely or never
    b. Occasionally
    c. Frequently
    d. Almost always

19. Do you feel the need to seek external validation or approval?

    a. Rarely or never
    b. Occasionally
    c. Frequently
    d. Almost always

20. Do you feel the need for things to be perfect and have difficulty accepting mistakes or flaws?

    a. Rarely or never
    b. Occasionally
    c. Frequently

d. Almost always

21. How often do you engage in negative self-talk?

    a. Rarely or never
    b. Occasionally
    c. Frequently
    d. Almost always

22. Do you struggle with feelings of guilt or shame?

    a. Rarely or never
    b. Occasionally
    c. Frequently
    d. Almost always

23. Do you have difficulty expressing your emotions or avoid talking about personal struggles?

    a. Rarely or never
    b. Occasionally
    c. Frequently
    d. Almost always

24. Do you often seek comfort or escape through excessive sleeping or napping?

    a. Rarely or never
    b. Occasionally
    c. Frequently
    d. Almost always

25. Do you engage in repetitive or compulsive behaviors or rituals?

    a. Rarely or never
    b. Occasionally

c. Frequently

d. Almost always

Scoring: Assign the following points to each response: Rarely or never—1 point, Occasionally—2 points, Frequently—3 points, Almost always—4 points. Total up all the points and use this guideline to gain insights into the potential relationship between behavioral patterns and chronic pain.

- 25-39: Minimal presence of behavioral patterns associated with chronic pain.
- 40-59: Mild to moderate presence of behavioral patterns associated with chronic pain.
- 60-79: Significant presence of behavioral patterns associated with chronic pain.
- 80-100: High presence of behavioral patterns associated with chronic pain.

In your journal, reflect on the insights you've gained by taking this quiz. How has your awareness about the connection between subconscious behavioral patterns and chronic pain changed? Going through this exercise and realizing that past traumas are influencing today's behaviors and health may be bringing up many emotions for you. If that is the case, please find a person you can trust to speak with, a friend or family member who loves you unconditionally, or seek professional guidance and support.

2. Connect with Your Inner Child

We all have a child within us, the essence of our younger self, who represents our childhood experiences, emotions, and innocence. This sweet child embodies who we are at our core and our most authentic selves. The inner child is curious, playful, has a sense of wonder and a deep capacity for joy, but may also carry unresolved pain, unmet needs, and fears. Connecting with and nurturing our inner child can help us heal wounds from the past, cultivate self-love and acceptance, and open a pathway to profound transformation.

You may want to display a picture of your child-self in a prominent place to help you maintain a loving connection with your inner child throughout your day, promote a feeling of peace, and create a stronger sense of wholeness. When you look at your inner child, send her love and convey a feeling of "I've got you now" loving support.

To connect with your inner child, you must slow down, get quiet, and allow them to be heard. To help you do that, here is a guided meditation designed to create a safe and nurturing space for your inner child to express themselves and receive the love and care they may have missed in the past. You can record yourself reading this meditation or download my recording from http://painfreeonpurpose.com/ or use the QR Code provided on page 158. Before you begin, get comfortable in your healing sanctuary and ensure you won't be disturbed for about 30 minutes. Have your journal ready to record insights gained from this experience.

Guided Meditation to Nurture Your Inner Child

Get yourself into your favorite meditation position, either sitting or lying down. Ensure you are comfortable and won't be disturbed.

Gently close down your beautiful eyes. Take a few deep, slow breaths through your nose and into your belly. Breathing in. Slowly breathing out. Notice the feel of the breath as it moves through your nostrils. The coolness of the air as you inhale. The warmth of the air as you exhale.

Continue breathing slowly, connecting your hearing to the sound of your breath.

If your mind wanders and your thoughts stray at any time throughout this meditation, simply come back with your focus on my voice and the instructions in the meditation.

Again, deep inhale. And slowly release. Another deep inhale. Exhale with a sigh, releasing anything that is ready to move out.

And one more deep inhale, breathing in peace. Hold and exhale with a sigh, releasing anything that is ready to move out through the breath. Let that go with the breath.

Just allow yourself to breathe.

Allow your body to relax. Breathe into any areas of tension, letting go and releasing.

Notice the support beneath you and let yourself melt into it. You are fully supported. You are fully relaxed. Feel yourself completely and fully relaxed.

Now bring your awareness to the heart area in the middle of your chest. Feel the warmth there. Imagine a soft, gentle energy radiating from your heart. Visualize this as a soft, glowing light surrounding your heart. This is a safe and nurturing space within you.

Now bring to your mind an image of you as a small child. Imagine this younger version of yourself is standing in front of you now. See the innocent and curious child you once were, radiating warmth and vulnerability. Notice the unique features, notice how this younger version of you is standing, notice the sparkle in the eyes.

Reach your hand toward this inner child in an invitation to come closer. Let your inner child know that they are cherished and protected. Notice your inner child tentatively moving toward you, seeking reassurance and trust. As your hands touch, notice a deep wave of love and compassion flowing between you.

Now, you tenderly embrace your inner child, letting them know you are here to provide love and protection, conveying the message "I've got you now."

Visualize a gentle, golden light surrounding both of you, enveloping both of you in unconditional love and healing energy. Feel this loving light permeating every part of your being ... you and your inner child ... bringing warmth, peace, and renewal.

Within this healing and protected space, encourage your inner child to express feelings. Create a space of acceptance and understanding for all the emotions that come forth. Listen with compassion and understanding. Respond with loving tenderness and reassurance.

Continue to let your inner child know that you are always there for them, ever supportive, that your love is unwavering, and that you face challenges together. Remind your inner child of their inherent worthiness and that they deserve love, happiness, and fulfillment of desires. Feel your inner child receive your love and reassurance.

Now, imagine that you both are engaging in an activity together that brings your inner child joy and delight. See both of you doing this activity together, smiling and feeling playful in this shared experience.

Take a moment to feel gratitude for your inner child, for the gifts this sweet child brings into your life. Feel innocence, playfulness, and joy wash over you, and give thanks for these uplifting gifts from your inner child.

When your playtime comes to a close, invite your inner child into the safe sanctuary of your heart. Let the spirit of your inner child merge with your present self, unifying in love within your heart. Knowing you are always together, always there for each other.

With a deep, long breath, feel gratitude in your heart for this time you have taken to connect with your inner child. Feel the deep healing, integration, and love that have been cultivated in this time together.

Gently bring your awareness back to your physical body, to the support beneath you, and your breath. Feel appreciation for the sense of peace and serenity within you.

When you are ready, you can very slowly open your beautiful eyes again. As you go about your day, you will carry this love and connection with your inner child with you. Know that you can create a connection with your inner child at any time, whenever you desire to feel love and nurturing.

Key Chapter Takeaways

- Thoughts, both conscious and subconscious, drive the nervous system.
- Repeated thoughts create beliefs which drive behaviors.
- 90% of thoughts and behaviors are on repeat.
- Most beliefs are formed before the age of seven.
- Fear about the pain and what it means can keep triggering the stress response.
- The biggest mistake people make is repeating the thoughts and behavior patterns that create nervous system dysregulation, perpetuating the pain.

Chapter 3

The Simple Solution to Pain Resolution

"Do the best you can, until you know better.
Then when you know better, do better."
—Maya Angelou

Your past is written all over your present. If you have chronic pain, something in your past has created a stress response in the body, and pain is there to let you know there is a problem. As we learned in Chapter 1, the body is always responding to the environment. When a threat is perceived, the nervous system will shift to the stress response, and if the threat continues, the body will no longer be in homeostasis. The threat may be from events and may come in the form of environmental toxins such as chemicals, microbes, and electromagnetic fields from our physical environment. We are built to deal with these threats, unless they are too much at once or they go on for too long. Prolonged or extreme stress can cause the nervous system to get stuck in the parasympathetic state, or nervous system dysregulation.

In Chapter 2, we learned that over time, it's the repeating thought patterns triggering the stress response of the nervous system that keep the body in protection mode and in pain. We also discussed how the brain, which is so good at learning, learns pain really well. Feeling fear about the pain increases neural networks in the brain for pain, increasing pain for protection, and perpetuating a pain-fear cycle.

The simple solution to pain resolution is to reprogram the brain for safety instead of fear. This can be accomplished with repeated practice of nervous system regulation techniques. It's not enough to do these practices once in a while. The brain needs consistent repetition to learn.

From riding a bicycle to playing a musical instrument, learning takes practice and commitment.

This is a simple solution. Simple, but not easy, right? Most people struggle with consistency and commitment. Additionally, most of our daily subconscious thoughts and behaviors are ingrained habits, and we know how hard it is to break old habits. Instead, the solution is to form new daily habits that support nervous system regulation.

When I came to this realization in my journey with pain, I knew my subconscious programs were deeply rooted and that I needed to understand the mind and how to change those subconscious programs. This led me to neuroscience, the study of the brain. I delved into the research around the brain and pain.

Lessons from Neuroscience

For many years, it was believed that the brain was not capable of creating new neurons beyond early adulthood. Now we know that the brain is neuroplastic, meaning the brain can rewire itself based on our thoughts, experiences, and emotions. This means that how we think and what we believe can quite literally reshape the brain's wiring, strengthening pathways that either reinforce pain or create relief.

In this light, it becomes very clear that pain is not merely physical. Instead, pain is a complex experience shaped by the brain's interpretation of sensory signals. When tissue injury occurs, pain receptors send signals to the brain, which then evaluates these messages in the context of emotions, memories, and beliefs. This evaluation determines the intensity and quality of the acute pain experience.

In chronic pain conditions, the brain's processing can become confused. Prolonged pain can lead to changes in brain structure and function, reinforcing pain pathways and making the sensation more persistent. This phenomenon is a testament to the brain's capacity to learn.

Pain that is felt not from ongoing tissue damage but from the brain's learned response to certain stimuli is called mind-body syndrome, neuroplastic pain, centrally sensitized pain, or, as named by Dr. John Sarno, tension myositis syndrome (TMS). Through neuroplasticity, the brain can develop and strengthen neural pathways associated with pain, even in the absence of a physical reason for the pain. This means that the brain can generate real pain sensations based on its previous experiences and learned associations. Fear and other negative thoughts and emotions, whether conscious or subconscious, play a pivotal role in this process.

Through the study of neuroscience, I discovered that the brain *learns* pain. The brain is so good at learning that it can keep those neural pathways for pain going, even when there's no longer a physical reason for the pain. If we keep repeating the thought patterns that send a message of fear to the brain, then the brain will perpetuate the pain. Instead, we can use the brain's neuroplasticity to learn a different response.

The Brain Can Unlearn Pain

The brain is our biggest ally when it comes to resolving chronic pain. To help us in our path to pain freedom, we can take advantage of the brain's incredible learning power and use that to our advantage. We can teach the brain to *unlearn* pain.

Alan Gordon is a therapist who developed Pain Reprocessing Therapy, a mind-body approach for chronic pain treatment. In his book *The Way Out*, Gordon explains how fear and stress reinforce chronic pain, stating: "When the brain experiences pain over and over, those neurons get 'wired together,' and they get better and better at firing together" (Gordon & Ziv, 2022). The brain is very good at learning new things; in this case, the brain is learning pain in response to perceived danger, which can be our thoughts about the pain itself. There's nothing like physical symptoms to get our attention, right? Naturally, we notice the pain and we begin to fear the pain and what it means to our future. Because we are hardwired from an evolutionary standpoint to notice fear, the brain pays even more attention to the pain. This causes more stress, and the brain turns on more pain for "protection." The brain gets confused and stuck in a pain-fear cycle and keeps wiring neurons for pain.

The good news is that because of neuroplasticity, you can rewire these patterns by consciously choosing thoughts that signal safety to your nervous system. Engaging in activities that foster a sense of safety, control, and well-being can help rewire the brain's pain pathways and release the need for pain. Techniques like mindfulness, breathwork, and visualization can recondition the subconscious to expect safety instead of threat. By learning how to harness the power of your conscious mind, you can gently guide your subconscious into a new reality that supports healing instead of reinforcing pain.

Research in neural retraining for pain relief is very promising. In the 2021 Boulder Back Pain study, 151 participants who had chronic back pain for more than ten years were divided into three groups. A third of them in the control group received the usual care, a third were given a placebo, and a third received eight one-hour sessions of Pain Reprocessing Therapy (PRT). After four weeks, 66 percent of the participants receiving PRT were nearly or fully pain-free, compared to just 10 percent of the control group. Nearly everyone receiving PRT, 98 percent, had at least some improvement, and these results were maintained a year later (Ashar et al., 2022).

Dr. Howard Schubiner, Director of the Mind Body Medicine Center in Michigan and author of *Unlearn Your Pain: A 28-Day Process to Reprogram Your Brain,* says that the vast majority of chronic pain cases have no structural issue. Instead, the brain has created neural pathways that help the brain remember pain and keep the cycle of pain going. The brain creates pain through a process called predictive processing.

Schubiner (2022) says, "The brain creates sensations it expects us to feel. When the brain is in an ongoing state of warning or danger, it will continue to create pain with movement, fatigue with activity, disordered thought processes, and many other sensations designed to enforce rest and inactivity. And the more the accompanying neural circuits are activated, the more they become normalized as default circuits."

By addressing the brain and nervous system dysregulation, helping the body return to a state of safety, it is possible to turn off the chronic pain response. To do this, we need to break the habit of pain and create a new habit of feeling safe and calm. Yes, unlearning pain is simply a matter of habit: what we consistently think and do over time so that the brain's neural pathways can be rewired. This is the simple solution to pain resolution, the foundational starting point to help release chronic pain. Once structural issues like injury, tumors, or infections are ruled out, pain can be addressed by retraining the brain and nervous system.

The Science of Habits

If we want to make a change, we must do things differently than we did before. As the saying goes, "The definition of insanity is doing the same thing over and over and expecting different results." Healing does not happen in one miraculous leap; rather, it's through consistent daily habits that support the body's natural ability to heal. When it comes to habits, it's what you do every day, not what you do occasionally, that really matters.

Coming back to the foundation of most chronic health conditions, a dysregulated nervous system, we will focus on taking actions to shift the nervous system to the parasympathetic state. These new actions will become the new habits that will regulate your nervous system. These habits are laid out in Part II, The DESIGN Blueprint. You will learn and do the twelve Healing Habits that will help you shift to nervous system regulation to create a state of healing in the body. Knowing which healing habits to cultivate is one thing. Making habits consistent so they stick is another. To do that, we must understand how habits form and how to make new habits stick. Before moving on to Part II, let's explore the science of habit formation to support you on your healing journey.

What are habits? Habits are behaviors we do automatically without having to think about them. Like computer programs, habits are the automatic behaviors that have been programmed into our subconscious mind. Driving a car, for example, has likely become so automatic that you may arrive at your destination with barely any recollection of the drive you took to get there. Our subconscious mind helps us get through day-to-day living by learning habits so that we don't have to think about the details of doing daily tasks. Some habits serve us well, like daily teeth brushing. Others don't serve us so well, like poor food choices, binge-watching, social media scrolling, gossiping, shopping, negative thinking, criticizing oneself, and others.

Once habits are programmed in our subconscious mind, changing them takes effort. Creating new habits, even when we know they will improve our lives, also takes effort.

In his book *Atomic Habits: An Easy & Proven Way to Build Good Habits & Break Bad Ones,* James Clear identifies four parts of a habit loop: cue, craving, response, and reward. Setting and maintaining good habits follow four fundamental and simple laws tied to each part of the habit loop. These laws are like levers that influence behavior. These simple laws are: make it obvious, make it attractive, make it easy, and make it satisfying (Clear, 2018). Let's consider each of these laws and how they are tied to the four parts of the habit loop.

1. **Make it obvious**: Have reminders to cue the habit, which could include a habit you already have.
2. **Make it attractive**: Make the new habit pleasurable or pair it with another pleasurable activity.

3. **Make it easy**: Friction prevents habits from forming, so reduce the friction with preparation.
4. **Make it satisfying**: The brain needs an incentive or immediate gratification, no matter how small.

In the DESIGN Blueprint, I'll integrate these concepts to help you create new healing habits to support nervous system regulation.

Bringing Your Healing Habits to Life

While understanding the foundational laws of habit formation is essential, truly integrating new habits into your life, especially when you're navigating chronic pain or health challenges, requires a compassionate, strategic approach. Think of these extra steps as the supportive structure that helps your healing habits take root and flourish. To help successfully integrate new healing habits, we'll consider some habit success strategies: be specific, habit stacking, rewards, and commitment.

Creating clarity around your habits gives them a stronger foundation. Instead of vague intentions like "I'll meditate more," try crafting a specific, actionable plan. Your brain thrives on clarity, and having a clear roadmap reduces decision fatigue. A simple framework to follow is: I will {ACTION}, at {TIME}, in {LOCATION}. For example, *I will practice heart-focused breathing at 8:00 a.m. in my healing sanctuary.* When you name exactly what you'll do, when you'll do it, and where it will happen, your chances of following through increase dramatically. This transforms a general intention into a concrete commitment.

One of the most effective ways to build a new habit is to link it to something you already do. This method, known as habit stacking, allows you to seamlessly weave new behaviors into your day without overwhelming your brain's capacity for change. Use this formula: After I {CURRENT HABIT}, I will {NEW HABIT}. For example: *After I brush my teeth in the morning, I will spend five minutes practicing gratitude.* Think of your current habit as an anchor that keeps the new habit steady and rooted, making it easier for the new habit to grow stronger over time.

Visual cues of progress, like a habit tracker, activate the brain's reward system, enhancing motivation and reinforcing positive behavior. Consider these strategies:

- Use a daily habit tracker, calendar, or simple checklist.
- Watch as your progress builds momentum through visible records of your achievements.
- Each checkmark becomes a small victory, a visual reminder that you're showing up for yourself and staying committed to your healing journey.
- Reward yourself for achieving milestones, such as a full week or month of consistent practice.

Accountability is another way to help establish new habits. This could be accountability with a coach, a group, or another person implementing the same habit. Another form of accountability is to publicly announce your intentions. If keeping your word is high on your personal value system, then making a public commitment to implementing a new habit can provide strong motivation to follow through on that habit.

When implementing new habits, it's important to be kind to yourself as you bring in new lifestyle changes. Changing habits isn't easy, so rather than striving for perfection, be compassionate with yourself if you stumble along the way.

Remember that establishing new habits takes time. Popular thinking was that it takes three weeks to learn a new habit; however, a seminal study in 2009 found that a new habit takes anywhere from 18 to 254 days to become automatic, with 66 days being the average (Lally et al., 2009). In 2021, another study used machine learning to analyze the habits of over 30,000 gymgoers over four years. The same study also examined handwashing habits of over 3,000 hospital workers over nearly 400 shifts. On average, it took six months for the gym habit to form and a few weeks for the handwashing to become a habit for the hospital workers (Calvin, 2023).

It's clear there's a wide variety of timelines when it comes to habit formation. We are all different, and you may find some habits easier than others to become automatic. As a general guideline for introducing new habits in Part II of this book, I suggest that you focus on one or two new habits until they become automatic for you, or practice them for at least 28 days before adding in another new habit. "Automatic" simply means that it becomes easier for you to do the habit than not to do it. Ultimately, you choose your pace. Just be aware of how you feel and if it feels like too much too fast, just slow down and remember that healing is about the tiny daily actions, and about focusing on progress, not perfection.

You Can Do This

Building new habits, particularly when healing from chronic pain, isn't about forcing yourself into rigid routines. Instead, it's about creating supportive structures that nurture your growth and well-being. Small, consistent actions lead to powerful transformations over time. Every step you take is a reminder of your strength and resilience. You are the hero of your own healing journey, and each positive habit leads you to the vibrant, pain-free life you deserve. With your help, your body can release protection and unlearn the habit of pain.

Heartwork

1. Journal Exercise: Mapping the Habit of Pain

This exercise will help you identify the specific habitual thought patterns and triggers that may be reinforcing your pain-fear cycle.

Instructions:

Begin by reflecting on the last time you experienced a pain flare-up. Answer the following prompts:

- **Trigger**: What was happening right before the pain intensified (e.g., specific thoughts, emotions, activities, or environments)?
- **Thoughts**: What thoughts ran through your mind at that moment? Were they fear-based (e.g., "This will never get better" or "I can't handle this pain")?
- **Emotions**: What emotions did you feel in response (fear, frustration, sadness)?
- **Behavior**: What actions did you take following the pain trigger (resting, canceling plans, avoiding movement)?
- **Reflection**: How might these reactions be reinforcing the pain-fear cycle?

End the journaling session by writing one compassionate affirmation that signals safety to your nervous system, for example, "I am safe, and my body knows how to heal."

2. Visualization Exercise: Rewiring for Safety and Calm

This guided visualization helps train the brain to associate safety, calm, and healing instead of fear and pain. You can do this exercise anytime, and it is especially helpful when you are experiencing pain. Before you begin, rate the intensity of pain you are experiencing out of ten, with 0 being no pain and 10 being the worst pain you could imagine.

Instructions:

- Find a quiet space where you won't be disturbed.
- Close your eyes and take a few deep, slow breaths to center yourself.

- Visualize your brain as a complex web of glowing pathways. Notice which pathways feel "lit up" by pain or fear.
- Now, imagine those pathways gently dimming, while new, brighter pathways emerge. These represent safety, calm, and healing.
- Picture yourself engaging in peaceful activities (e.g., walking in nature, connecting with loved ones, or feeling the warmth of the sun). As you do, mentally affirm: "I am safe. My body remembers how to heal."
- End with three deep breaths, feeling gratitude for the healing process already beginning within you.

After you've finished, rate the pain again. You should notice a reduction in pain intensity. At the very least, you should feel calmer, which will have a physical benefit because the nervous system will shift to the relaxation response.

This practice reinforces the feeling of safety in the nervous system and supports neuroplasticity by training the brain to associate new emotional responses with comfort and calm. You can also go to http://painfreeonpurpose.com/ or use the QR Code provided on page 158 to download an audio version of this visualization exercise.

Key Chapter Takeaways

- The simple solution to pain resolution is to consistently repeat patterns to train the brain and nervous system for safety until they become new habits.
- Take advantage of the brain's neuroplasticity and incredible capacity to learn new things and teach it to unlearn pain.
- New research in pain science indicates that most chronic pain can be resolved with brain retraining.
- Apply the science of learning new habits to making new healing habits stick.
- Learning new habits takes repetition, time, and commitment.

PART II:
The DESIGN Blueprint

Chapter 4

Overview of the DESIGN Blueprint

"The best way to predict the future is to create it."
—Abraham Lincoln

There are two ways to live your life: by default or by design. Living by default is reactionary, and it's likely you've already been living mostly that way. That's the way I lived for the first fifty years of my life. Becoming pain-free on purpose means that you are living life by design.

As an engineer, I designed foundations and structures for buildings. Every design needed a blueprint to clarify the vision and help bring that vision to life. Imagine the confusion and subpar outcome if a building were constructed without clarifying the design on a blueprint. There would be an incredible waste of precious time and resources. Similarly, cultivating the version of yourself capable of transcending a health condition requires a blueprint—a roadmap—for a deliberate trajectory toward freedom.

Through my personal journey and working with many people, I've developed a proven six-step methodology I call the DESIGN Blueprint. The DESIGN Blueprint is not just a collection of steps but a transformative process, an invitation to become the version of yourself that allows healing to happen by connecting the mind, body, and spirit. Each letter in the word DESIGN stands for a vital step in this journey: Desire, Explore, Surrender, Integrate, Generate, and Navigate. This blueprint provides a path that has already helped thousands of people find freedom from pain and discover the potential within themselves.

Just as every engineering project is different, so is each person's path to wellness. The DESIGN Blueprint will guide you through a process that fosters an interconnectedness of body, mind, and spirit to activate the body's natural healing ability. Genuine healing is underpinned by profound self-love. There is no need to rush through this process. In the words of mindset and visionary, Mary Morrissey, "Baby steps will take you anywhere as long as you keep taking them."

The DESIGN Blueprint is the core teaching of my Calm by DESIGN mentorship, Living Pain-Free membership and You Can Heal self-study course. These are the simple steps that work. Let's have a brief look at each step in the DESIGN Blueprint.

Step 1: Desire

The first step on the DESIGN Blueprint is about embracing your deepest desires. Your desires come from your soul, and this step will help you fulfill your soul's desires. When you follow your soul's desires, you will feel compelled to take inspired action, trust the process, and surrender to the flow. Not following your desires may well be why your body has spoken to you with chronic pain.

When a health challenge comes along, of course, it may seem that the obvious desire is to be healthy again. Instead of focusing on healing your body, what we are talking about in this step is what you would do if you had vibrant health again. Would you travel, and where would you travel? Would you play with your children or grandchildren? Would you enjoy walking again or climbing a mountain?

This step will help you get very clear on what you yearn for, and what it looks and feels like to have your wishes fulfilled, and the habits will help reprogram your subconscious mind to support your desires. Knowing what your desires are will not only help keep you motivated as you create new ways of living, but the feelings you will cultivate will draw that desire towards you like a magnet.

Getting in touch with your desires is an intentional process. To really tune in to the whispers of your soul, you need to create moments of stillness to slow down the chatter of the mind and help you tune in to your desires. By creating a calm mind, you also create a calm body to support your desires.

Step 2: Explore

The second step on the DESIGN Blueprint, Explore, is about aligning your mind and body with your true self. You'll explore how your physiology responds when you change how you think, and you'll connect to feelings in the body. Your body has been speaking to you, asking for your help. It's time for you to listen, by choosing new thoughts and beliefs to help you stay focused on and in alignment with your desires. Approach this step with curiosity about what happens when you begin to support your body, which really means listening to the little voice inside that knows you've been hard on yourself for far too long.

Your body is your vehicle to express your true self in this life experience. Manifesting illness is simply a message that you have not been in alignment with your soul. It's time to make a change. We do this by creating awareness around thoughts and connecting with feelings in the body to align both with the true loving essence of who you really are. Anything other than this is a result of conditioned programming learned throughout life.

Step 3: Surrender

The third step of the DESIGN Blueprint, Surrender, is about letting go of what's not serving you. Here, we release the rational, controlling, thinking mind and tune in to the wisdom of the body. Surrender is often associated with "giving up" or a feeling of resignation. The meaning of surrender in this step is emotional and physical surrender. This means letting go of the mind's need to keep pushing rather than passive resignation. It also means understanding that all our experiences are happening *for* us, not *to* us, and accepting that what we perceive as negative experiences reveal where we can create more freedom.

Michael Singer, author of *The Untethered Soul,* has wisely said, "Surrender is the ultimate technique. It's not something that you do; it's something that you stop doing."

Surrender is also about letting go of outcomes. In the wise words of Marianne Williamson, "Surrender means, by definition, giving up attachment to results. When we let go of attachment, we open ourselves to all possibilities." Trusting the process of life is the opposite of what most of us have been taught to do, but through surrender, we can tune in to the wisdom of our soul, which is all-knowing and has access to far more information than the rational mind. Through surrender, the body can release the protections it has built up over time.

Step 4: Integrate

The fourth step in the DESIGN Blueprint, Integrate, invites you to align with your body's natural intelligence, honoring its profound ability to heal and thrive when given the building blocks it needs. By nourishing your body, reducing toxins, and creating a clean, supportive environment, you allow its innate wisdom to flourish. This step is about recognizing the sacred partnership between you and your body, working with its signals, respecting its needs, and trusting its capacity for healing. Through small, intentional choices, you can create the optimal conditions for your body to function at its highest potential, bringing balance, vitality, and a deeper connection to your true self.

Step 5: Generate

The Generate step is about actively cultivating energy in your life by engaging with the world around you in ways that bring joy, connection, and vitality. This is where the physical and the spiritual intersect, through joyful movement, loving relationships, and intentional choices that nourish your body, mind, and spirit. By embracing physical movement and connections that uplift and energize you, you create the momentum needed to support your healing journey. Generating energy is not just about physical vitality; it's about aligning in harmony with the flow of life and embodying the vibrancy that empowers transformation and growth.

Step 6: Navigate

The final step in the DESIGN Blueprint, Navigate, invites you to embrace playfulness and expansion as essential elements of living a fulfilling life. Your soul instinctively seeks exploration, creativity, and growth, but in the whirlwind of daily responsibilities, these vital aspects of self-expression can often take a backseat. Navigate encourages you to reconnect with the joy of curiosity and the thrill of discovery. Through these experiences, your nervous system can relax because you are engaging in life in a fulfilling way.

This step prompts you to ask yourself, *What truly brings me joy?* and *What sparks my curiosity?* By pursuing these answers, you honor your authentic self and create space for a life of deeper meaning and connection. When you navigate with intention, you align with the flow of life, welcoming new opportunities and experiences that expand your horizons and nurture your soul.

Each step on the DESIGN Blueprint is represented on this graphic.

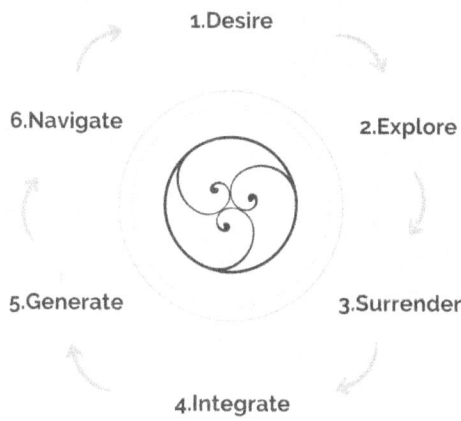

You'll notice that the DESIGN Blueprint is circular. After you've gone through the Blueprint, you'll likely have discovered a new desire you'd like to follow as your body heals and you are ready to expand. Nature itself is expansive, and so are you!

Becoming pain-free using the DESIGN Blueprint is simply a matter of habit. It's the day-to-day choices we make and how we live our lives. This is simple and profound at the same time.

We know from research that nearly all chronic health conditions are a result of lifestyle habits. To get different results, we need to change habits to ones that will create an environment in which the body can heal. There is plenty of research on habits that support healing, and most of us know what we *should* do, yet we don't do it. Why? Because creating new habits takes effort, most people aren't applying the habit success strategies mentioned in Chapter 3.

But you, my friend, are different! By following the DESIGN Blueprint, you will successfully implement the habits that will help your body heal.

For each step on the DESIGN Blueprint, you'll incorporate two Healing Habits. Each of these habits could be a book in itself, and there are already many books written on all these topics. My goal isn't to provide you with the supporting evidence for each of these, but to get you moving forward using proven tools and strategies.

The twelve Healing Habits you'll implement on the DESIGN Blueprint are:

1. Create Calm
2. Amplify Your Vision
3. Manage Your Mind
4. Generate Love
5. Sleep and Rest
6. Forgive and Release
7. Nourish Thyself
8. Embrace Natural Living
9. Find Your Friends
10. Move with Joy
11. Play and Create
12. Learn, Grow, and Expand

To help you be successful as you bring in the new habits, I'll support you by guiding you on how to apply the habit success strategies we learned in Chapter 3. You'll find a useful *Healing Habit Tracker* in the Resources at the end of this book. You can also download a PDF version at http://painfreeonpurpose.com/ or use the QR Code provided on page 158.

These may seem like a lot, but remember, you're going to take this one step at a time. In the following chapters, I'll guide you through the DESIGN Blueprint, helping you implement the twelve Healing Habits that will shift you toward vitality and health again. You can do this, my friend! Let's get started on Step 1, Desire.

Chapter 5

Step 1: Desire

"The person without a purpose is like a ship without a rudder."
—Thomas Carlyle

Step 1 of the DESIGN Blueprint, Desire, is a foundational step in the healing process. It's about creating moments of calm and getting clear on what you desire. From a place of calm stillness, you'll visualize your healed and healthy self, doing something you love, and then generate the feelings that match that desire. Your desire to be well and live a vibrant, healthy life comes from deep within your soul. On some level, those desires have been denied in your life. It's time to honor and embrace the you that you came here to be.

In the Desire step, you will implement the first two Healing Habits and make them a daily practice. The two habits for Desire are:

- Habit #1: Create Calm
- Habit #2: Amplify Your Vision

Let's learn about these habits and get you started.

Healing Habit #1: Create Calm

Getting in touch with your desire to be whole and healthy requires moments of calm throughout the day to relax the nervous system as a foundational aspect of supporting the body's natural healing processes. Building a daily mindfulness practice with the intention to create calm will help you make the shift to become empowered in your healing.

Mindfulness is simply being fully present where you are, without ruminating over the past or worrying about the future. When we think of mindfulness, what often comes to mind is a person sitting cross-legged, with eyes closed, deep in meditation. Mindfulness, however, need not fit that stereotype. This can be as simple as focusing on the breath, listening to a guided meditation or visualization exercise, or sitting silently and simply noticing what you're noticing and letting thoughts drift away.

Jon Kabat-Zinn popularized mindfulness-based stress reduction (MBSR) in the 1970s to help people cope with stress, pain, and other health conditions. In his 2013 book, *Full Catastrophe Living*, Kabat-Zinn wrote that after eight weeks of MBSR plus home practice of meditation, 72% of patients received at least a 33% reduction in PRI (Pain Rating Index) and 61% received at least a 50% reduction in PRI (Kabat-Zinn, 1990). Over the last fifty years, numerous studies have demonstrated that various mindfulness practices, including meditation, breathwork (deliberately controlling the breath), yoga, qigong, Tai Chi, and others are associated with improved mental health, longevity, and relationships, lowered blood pressure, reduction in symptoms across a myriad of health conditions, and less pain. Many business titans tout a mindfulness practice as part of their formula for success!

With so much compelling evidence, it's clear that making time to create calm each day is a necessary resiliency tool and imperative for anyone interested in healing. For this Healing Habit, we are going to begin with the most foundational mindfulness practice of them all: breathwork. Breathing is necessary for life, but breathing can also be used as a tool for healing. The quickest way to switch the nervous system to the parasympathetic, or rest-and-digest, state is with conscious breathing, and this can be achieved in minutes.

I have found breathwork to be incredibly powerful as I was healing, and it continues to be a resiliency tool I use in everyday life. Simply making time to focus on the breath automatically slows down my rate of breathing and shifts me to calm. It's my number one go-to tool. We always have the breath with us, right? This makes breathwork the ultimate portable device for nervous system relaxation, and it's totally free.

We all breathe, of course, but *how* you breathe can send different signals to the nervous system. Numerous studies have shown that to calm the nervous system, it's best to breathe through the nose, into the lower lungs, with long, slow exhales. When most people focus on breathing consciously, they begin with an inhale, but this isn't helpful if they are habitually breathing into the chest. Instead, start by pulling the belly toward the spine as far as you can manage as you slowly exhale. Then inhale through the nose, pushing the belly out again before filling the upper part of the lungs. On the exhale, slowly, slowly release air from the upper lungs and then the lower belly, pulling the belly back toward the spine. It may be helpful to place one hand on your lower belly and the other on the chest so you can feel the movement there. Initially, if you're not used to belly breathing, this breathwork practice will require concentration and may not feel relaxing. If you feel stressed at any time, then simply breathe normally and just notice your breathing. Simply notice the feel of the breath as it moves in and out of the body. Often, this act of observing the breath will automatically slow down your breathing. You could count your breathing: about five or six seconds for the inhale and five or six seconds for the exhale, pausing slightly in between. Gradually, you could extend the length of the exhale, making the exhale longer than the inhale.

Do this practice of creating calm with mindful breathing for at least three minutes, three times each day. You can set a timer for three minutes or play peaceful music to guide you. There are several free meditation apps to help you create calm. You can choose peaceful music and start and finish bells for whatever length of time you choose.

You may already be doing other, more advanced breathwork or meditation practices, and if so, you can use this Healing Habit to make time to practice one of those instead. The important thing is to create calm by focusing on the breath for at least three minutes, three times per day or more.

The time of day is important. How you start your day has an impact on your entire day, which is why practicing in the morning is essential. This also gives you a sense of accomplishment to help add momentum as you begin implementing new habits. You could practice this habit in bed right after you wake up in the morning, or whenever works best for you. I like to do my morning practice in my Healing Sanctuary. I feel more peaceful the moment I sit down there. I introduced you to the Healing Sanctuary in the Heartwork of Chapter 1. Did you create yours yet? If not, now is the time to do that, my friend.

Your midday practice could be tied to your lunch hour, or at any time in the middle of the day that works for you. If you choose to connect this habit with lunchtime, you could do it after you sit down, before you eat. This will also help with digestion because your nervous system will be more relaxed. You could simply sit quietly at any point in your day. Whenever you decide to do your midday practice, what matters is that you are consistently dedicating time during the middle of the day to create calm.

Before going to bed at night, you want to reset your mind and body for calm. Your evening practice could be before you get into bed as a wind-down routine. Or you could create calm right after you turn off the light, before you fall asleep. Becoming more peaceful before sleep will help relax your nervous system, allowing you to sleep better.

Recall from Chapter 3 James Clear's four laws for forming new habits: make it obvious, make it attractive, make it easy, and make it satisfying.

Thinking about these laws, how can you make creating calm three times a day easier to implement? To make it obvious, you could set reminders on your phone, or place Post-It notes in places where you'll see them, or you could use a picture or an object as a reminder. To make it attractive, you can be aware of how good it feels to feel calm and notice that the more you do it, the better you feel. To make it easy, tie this habit to something you are already doing each day, and do this new habit either right before or right after something you already do. To make it satisfying, reward yourself every time you practice creating calm by checking off a box on the Healing Habit Tracker in the Resources at the end of this book, or go to http://painfreeonpurpose.com/ or use the QR Code provided on page 158 to download a PDF version. You may have your own calendar or journal where you track your progress. You could also give yourself a milestone reward after practicing consistently for a week or a month, for example.

I also want to remind you, as you bring in this habit and all the others in the DESIGN Blueprint, that the goal isn't perfection. Good enough might mean on some days, you practice only once, or you might even miss a day or a few days altogether. That's OK. Remind yourself that you are human, and humans are perfectly imperfect. Be kind to yourself, and remember what you *have* done, then just get back on track again. If you think the Healing Habit Tracker activates perfectionist tendencies, then, by all means, feel free not to use it. The primary goal with any tracking system is to activate the reward centers in the brain to support positive behavior change.

Summary of Healing Habit #1: Create Calm

- Get into a comfortable position and relax your body.
- Set a timer for three minutes, or longer, or play peaceful music to guide you.
- Close your eyes and exhale by pulling the belly toward the spine.

- Inhale through the nose, first pushing the belly out to fill the lower lungs, then the upper lungs.
- Exhale slowly, releasing air from the upper lungs first, then the lower lungs by pulling the belly back toward the spine, letting the exhale be longer than the inhale.
- Repeat until the timer ends. Keep your attention on feeling the movement of air in the body, feeling gratitude for the abundance of air available to you.
- Practice this habit three times a day, each morning, midday, and prior to sleep.
- On your Healing Habit Tracker, check off a box each time you practice this habit.

Healing Habit #2: Amplify Your Vision

We've all heard about the power of visualization. Athletes have known about this and have practiced mental imagery for years to improve performance by visualizing their success ahead of time. The practice of visualization has spilled over to leadership, business, personal development, and health.

Visualization is one of the primary methods used in sports psychology to improve athletic performance. Along with visualizing a perfect performance in every detail, when athletes create powerful emotions to go with the mental imagery and intensify those emotions, the visualizations are more powerful. Michael Phelps, the greatest Olympian swimmer of all time, would visualize every detail of swimming a successful race, developing a habit of success. He said, "No matter what little thing goes wrong, I have already prepared for it thousands of times in my mind. I am ready for anything."

Studies have shown that the brain does not distinguish between an image coming through the optic nerve and an image created by thought alone. Comparing neurons in the brain when subjects looked at an image versus recalling the image in their "mind's eye," 88% of the same neurons were fired (Kreiman, 2000). In other words, the brain interprets imagined images in nearly the same way as real images we see with our eyes.

By visioning clearly on a regular basis, the brain's reticular activating system (RAS) will work to make that vision a reality. The brain must continually filter out what the subconscious mind has deemed "unimportant." Since the subconscious mind does not know the difference between a real and imagined image, creating visions of a desirable future is like planting seeds of what's important in the subconscious mind. Information that supports that vision will be filtered as "important," helping it become a reality. Your brain will help you take actions that support your vision.

Mental visualization and rehearsal can also result in physical changes in the body, including muscle strength. In one study, subjects were divided into three groups: one group was instructed to do strength training of the little finger for 12 weeks, 15 minutes per day, five days per week. The second group was instructed to "mentally" do the same training, while the third group did nothing and served as a control. The study found that the group that did the physical training had increased finger strength by 53% over the 12-week period. The control group had no increase in strength. The group that did the exercises mentally had a 35% increase in finger strength (Ranganathan, 2004). Simply imagining doing the exercises, while not as impactful as actually doing the exercises, still resulted in a physical change in the body.

The real power in visioning is through the feelings we create in the body while we are thinking about our future. Feelings are visceral vibrations in the body. Negative emotions such as grief, sadness, frustration, disappointment, apathy, anger, and jealousy are felt as lower vibrational feelings in the body. You might sense these as a feeling of "heaviness." Positive emotions like peace, happiness, joy, love, and exhilaration generate higher vibrational feelings in the body. When you think of things that generate these feelings, what do you feel? Do you sense a feeling of lightness or expansion?

Numerous studies have shown the connection between emotions and the autonomic nervous system. The research is clear: positive emotions are associated with nervous system regulation.

Through visioning and cultivating positive emotions along with the vision, we have the power to shift our vibrational frequency toward healing. By consciously cultivating positive thoughts and emotions, we can elevate our vibration and create an environment that supports healing. Visioning ourselves engaging in activities that bring us joy, practicing mindfulness, and seeking positive influences all contribute to this shift.

Early on in my healing journey, I would vision myself on the summit of Gros Morne Mountain, the second-highest peak on the island of Newfoundland, where I live. Many years before, I had hiked the eighteen-kilometer trail that led to the summit, so I was aware of how difficult the trail was, particularly how hard it was on the knees on the downhill section. I knew I had a long way to go from being barely able to walk around the block, but every day I would imagine myself reaching the summit and holding my arms up in victory, taking in the beautiful views, noticing the sun on my skin, feeling and hearing the wind, smelling the salty sea air, and feeling exhilaration in my body. While I sat there with my eyes closed, I could see, feel, hear, smell, and taste being on that summit. It felt so real to me. Sometimes, I would even raise my arms in the air in victory, as if I were there. It was like playing a virtual reality movie in my mind.

After I'd been doing this visualization for a while, I remembered hearing about the power of music to evoke strong emotions. Movie producers understand this concept well and use music to help create the feelings they want the audience to experience while watching the movie. Imagine a movie without the soundtrack. It would be a completely different experience! So, I added music to my visioning practice. I chose "The Climb" by Miley Cyrus. For me, the lyrics of this song are about physically climbing the mountain, but also the metaphor of my journey of overcoming the pain and the struggles I was facing along the way. The words reminded me to keep the faith, that eventually I would get there. I would literally get tears in my eyes as I listened to this song while imagining myself at the peak of Gros Morne, and I still do. I just played "The Climb" as I was writing this for you, and there were tears again!

As I held on to this vision and rehearsed it daily, I steadily improved. I went from barely walking to chair dancing to walking around the garden, then walking around the block. I started doing shorter hikes, then longer ones. Eventually, four years after the onset of rheumatoid arthritis, I climbed to the peak of Gros Morne, and I felt the exhilaration, just as I had envisioned! Over and over, students in my Living Pain-Free membership and Calm by DESIGN mentorship program see their visions come to fruition. Visioning works!

Now, it's your turn. Let's suspend logic for a bit and wave a magic wand. What if you were completely healthy and strong in your body? What is something you'd love to do that you can't do now, or you've been putting off because you're waiting to get well? Maybe it's playing with your grandchildren, traveling to a place you've always wanted to go, or doing an activity you aren't doing now. Think of an activity that would be fun for you that you're missing out on now. Envision yourself doing that activity and notice the feelings you have in your body.

If you've been ill for a long time, it might be hard to imagine yourself well, or doing so may feel unrealistic. It might be helpful to remember the wise words of Norman Vincent Peale, the author of *The Power of Positive Thinking*, who said, "Formulate and stamp indelibly on your mind a mental picture of yourself as succeeding. Hold this picture tenaciously and never permit it to fade. Your mind will seek to develop this picture!" Give yourself permission to just playfully imagine.

Once you've imagined your vision, write it down so you can easily recall it. Keep it short and succinct, about five or six sentences. Write this by hand since this helps reinforce the vision in your mind by activating different neural pathways in the brain. As you read over what you've written, notice if there's one emotion that stands out. For my vision on Gros Morne, the predominant emotion was exhilaration. Yours might be love, joy, courage, support, fearlessness, awe, gratitude, peace, playfulness, or any other positive emotion. Pick one emotion to focus on.

After you've identified the one emotion, notice where you feel that emotion in your body. This visceral experience of feeling an emotion in your body is important, so don't be tempted to skip over it. Remember that feelings are vibrations, and every cell in your body will feel your vibration. If you have trouble feeling the emotion in your body or if it's barely noticeable, that's okay. Just get still, focus, and keep practicing, and eventually you'll feel it. It may be helpful to say to yourself, *If I could feel this emotion in my body, where would I feel it?* An answer may surprise you.

Next, choose a song that elevates your chosen emotion. If a song doesn't immediately come to mind, you could do a search for "songs about ..." and see what comes up. Pick just one song, rather than making a playlist. You can always change your song, so there's no pressure to find *exactly* the right one.

To amplify your vision even further, you could add a physical action while you're playing your vision in your mind. For example, I mentioned that I raised my arms in victory. This helped me feel like I was physically there. Think about your vision and a small action you could do that represents your vision in action. This could be as simple as high-fiving yourself in the mirror for accomplishing your goal.

Finally, smile while you're visioning—you may not be able to help yourself! Smiling, even if it's fake, activates pleasure centers in the brain (Cross et al., 2023), and this will help make your vision feel even better.

This habit is not about trying to convince yourself that you're already healed. It's about creating positive expectations in your mind, which will reinforce the thoughts and behaviors that support your body's natural ability to heal. Remember that the mind creates the body. Let's get the mind working to help you feel good, and healing will happen as a happy side effect.

Here's how to put your amplified vision into action. While playing your power song, close your eyes and review your vision in your mind. Feel the emotion in your body as you do this. You may even feel tears welling up as you feel the strong positive emotion. Add in your small physical action.

Do this first thing in the morning, midday, and before going to bed. In the transition from waking to sleep, the brain shifts to a theta state, where it is very suggestible. By aligning your predominant thoughts with your desires right before sleep, you'll help reprogram your subconscious mind toward achieving those desires. If your song isn't accessible at any of these practice times, then just spend three minutes or so amplifying your vision without playing the song. After a while, you'll likely hear the song on repeat in your mind!

Summary of Healing Habit #2: Amplify Your Vision

- Pick one thing you would love to do that you are unable to do now. Envision yourself doing that. Tie in all your senses as if you were there.

- Write a description of your vision in five or six sentences.
- Choose one emotion that represents your vision and notice where you feel that emotion in your body.
- Choose one song that represents your vision and save it on a device.
- Choose a small physical action that represents your vision.
- Amplify your vision by listening to your song while reviewing your vision in your mind, feeling the emotions in your body, and doing the small physical action, first thing in the morning, midday, and prior to sleep.

Like Healing Habit #1, the goal is to practice Healing Habit #2 three times each day: morning, midday, and prior to sleep. Practice amplifying your vision right after creating calm. You can work on implementing Healing Habit #2 after Healing Habit #1 becomes automatic, or bring in both new habits at the same time. Choose what works best and is easiest for you. The first habit will cue the second habit, making it obvious. To make it attractive, you can really notice those positive feelings in your body—it feels good to feel good! To make it easy, have your song easily available to play on a portable device. To make it satisfying, reward your brain by checking off a box on the Healing Habit Tracker every time you practice, or use some other form of tracking your visioning practice.

Milestones for Step 1: Desire

- Healing Habit #1: Create Calm each morning, midday, and prior to sleep.
- Healing Habit #2: Amplify Your Vision each morning, midday, and prior to sleep.

This step is complete when you have incorporated each of these habits on a daily basis with consistency until each becomes automatic for you.

Practicing these habits at least three times a day will help reprogram your mind, both the conscious and subconscious mind, with positive emotions to support your intention and feel optimistic about your desired future.

Recall from Chapter 3 that new habits can take anywhere from 18 to 254 days to form, and 66 days is the average. As a guideline, practice any new habit for at least 28 days, then assess where you are. If this new habit feels well-established, then you're ready to add another habit. If not, then continue until it feels like it is an "automatic" part of your day.

Remember that you don't have to be perfect! What you do most of the time is what matters, so you're aiming to practice these habits every day, *most of the time*, until they are a regular part of your day and become automatic, or for at least 28 days. Once you are doing that, or when you feel ready, you can move on to step 2, Explore before you move on, reward yourself for completing the Desire step. Celebrate how you've been honoring your soulful desires by treating yourself in some way.

Chapter 6

Step 2: Explore

"The mind is everything. What you think you become."
—Buddha

Congratulations on implementing the Healing Habits of Step 1. Well done, my friend! You are likely noticing that your future feels more positive, and you're beginning to feel better. Take a moment to celebrate that and your commitment to yourself. Now you are ready to move on to the Explore step, where you'll align your thoughts and feelings to support nervous system regulation for healing. You'll create alignment through consistent practice of reprogramming your thoughts and creating moments of feeling loving presence throughout the day. The two healing habits for this step are:

- Healing Habit #3: Manage Your Mind
- Healing Habit #4: Generate Love

Let's learn about these two habits so you can begin implementing them as part of your daily practice.

Healing Habit #3: Manage Your Mind

Deepak Chopra has said, "The body is a reflection of your thoughts. If you change your thoughts, you change your body." If we want to make changes to our physical bodies, then we must begin with the mind. As we learned earlier, the mind runs the body's physiology through the central nervous system, changing our chemistry and physiology. To make the desired changes, we must devote awareness and intention to managing our day-to-day thoughts.

Healing Habit #3 will help create thoughts and beliefs to help instill a sense of safety in the subconscious mind, shift the autonomic nervous system into the relaxation response, and support the body's natural healing abilities. There are many ways to reprogram the subconscious mind for safety, but we will focus on one powerful practice you can do yourself.

Managing the Mind with Affirmations

One way to shift your nervous system out of the stress response and into the relaxation response is to reprogram the subconscious mind through repetition of affirmations. An affirmation is a statement that describes a goal as if it has already been achieved. These statements can be used to change your internal self-talk so that it is more in line with your goals. As we've already discussed, the brain is very good at learning new habits through repetition. For this habit, we are focusing on retraining the brain to focus on new thoughts and beliefs that support healing with self-affirmations.

Jack Canfield, co-author of the *Chicken Soup for the Soul* books and author of *The Success Principles*, recommends these guidelines when writing affirmations:

- **Start with the words "I am ..."** The subconscious mind interprets these two words as a command, so whatever you say after these is a directive to your brain.
- **Use the present tense.** Describe what you want as though it is already a reality.
- **State it in the positive.** The subconscious mind does not hear the words "no" or "not"; it will only hear what follows them because those images will form in the brain. So, always state the positive of what you want to achieve.
- **Keep it brief.** Keep the affirmation short enough so that it is easily remembered.

- **Make it specific.** Use specific outcomes rather than vague outcomes.
- **Use an action word ending in "ing".** Using a verb adds power to the affirmation and creates an image of the thing actually happening.
- **Include a dynamic feeling word.** By including the desired emotional state, you are connecting your thoughts to your feelings for even greater success. Examples are joyfully, happily, proudly, calmly, peacefully, delightedly, enthusiastically, lovingly, serenely, and triumphantly.
- **Make affirmations for yourself, not others.** You can't control anyone else's behavior, so your affirmations should describe your behavior, not another's.
- **Add "or something better" at the end, if appropriate.** There may be something better available to us than our limited experiences or beliefs allow us to conceive. Adding this statement allows for even more possibilities (Canfield, 2015).

Affirmations for Healing

Long before the onset of pain, I had learned about the power of affirmations for personal mastery. I knew that affirmations can be an incredibly powerful tool in changing self-talk. In fact, several studies have shown that affirmations can "restore self-competence by allowing individuals to reflect on sources of self-worth, such as core values" (Cascio, 2016). The underlying mechanism of the success of using self-affirmations for behavior change lies in the brain. Affirmations increase neural activity, as identified with fMRI imaging, in key regions of the brain's self-processing and valuation systems. Affirmations activate feelings, and feelings are the hidden drivers of behavior.

During the deep grief I was experiencing after my mother passed, I used affirmations to help pull me out. When my health challenge came along, again I turned to affirmations. Here is a list of affirmations I've used to support my health and healing, and now, thousands of others, too. Look over each of these and notice how they make you feel. Make a note of those that instill a strong positive feeling in your body. If you don't notice a strong feeling, then notice the ones that feel true and believable for you now.

- *I am enjoying health and vitality flowing to me with ease.*
- *I am safe in this moment.*
- *My health and vitality are getting stronger and stronger each day.*
- *It is safe for me to be healthy.*
- *I am confidently aware that every day and in every way, my health is getting better and better.*
- *I give myself permission to be healthy.*
- *I am happily enjoying the freedom of being in the best physical health of my life.*
- *I am brimming with energy and overflowing with joy.*
- *I am sending loving energy to every cell in my body.*
- *I am happily taking loving care of my body.*
- *I am allowing the intelligence of my body to do its healing work naturally.*
- *I appreciate how my body is always doing its best to create perfect health.*
- *I am enjoying the foods that are best for my body.*
- *I am allowing my body to heal itself each day.*
- *I am constantly discovering new ways to improve my health.*
- *I love and approve of myself.*
- *I am seeking out clues left by others to help me achieve my goals.*
- *I am in the best physical, emotional, and mental health of my life.*
- *My life gets better and better every day.*

- *I am brimming with energy and overflowing with joy.*
- *I am the architect of my life; I build its foundation and choose its contents.*
- *I am making choices in my life that are best for my body, mind, and spirit.*
- *My life is turning out better than I expected.*
- *I am confidently aware that everything is happening for my ultimate good.*
- *I am laying down powerful blueprints in my subconscious mind to make my dreams for health and vitality come true.*
- *My intuition is guiding me to make the best choices for my health.*
- *I love being in the flow of health and vitality.*
- *Creative ideas for health and wellness flow to me every day.*
- *I am at peace with my body.*
- *The more I look after my body, the more it looks after me.*
- *My body is an amazing self-correcting organism.*
- *It is my birthright to be healthy.*
- *My body is always supporting me.*
- *My genes are expressing themselves in positive ways.*
- *I love how easily my body heals itself.*
- *I am so blessed.*
- *I am the best version of myself today.*
- *I am grateful for the opportunities that allow me to be healthy.*
- *I love to eat food that is worthy of me.*
- *I am filled with gratitude for all that my body does for me.*
- *Every day and in every way, I am getting healthier and healthier.*
- *I give thanks for my increasing health.*
- *My body is constantly recreating itself in healthy new ways.*
- *I am a fountain of wellness.*
- *I am grateful for this day and the opportunities that open for me.*
- *I give thanks for all that is and all that is coming to me.*

- *I love all the good I can do in the world when I am healthy.*
- *I love feeling how I am getting stronger every day.*
- *My intuition guides me to make better choices every day.*
- *I trust the inner wisdom of my body.*
- *My body is truly a healing miracle.*
- *I express myself completely.*
- *My attitude of gratitude helps me heal.*
- *I love being healthy and strong.*
- *I appreciate all that my body does for me each day.*
- *I express the joy of living.*
- *I radiate wellness.*
- *I am vital, strong, and healthy.*
- *Every cell in my body is working for my health.*
- *I make decisions that guide me closer and closer to perfect health.*
- *I am secure and nourished by life.*
- *I allow myself to enjoy every moment.*
- *Life loves supporting me.*
- *I believe all things are possible for me.*
- *My health comes from listening to and acting upon my intuition.*
- *I believe in miracles.*
- *My vitality is constantly increasing.*
- *I believe all things are possible for me.*
- *My health is constantly improving.*
- *I am so grateful that my health is constantly improving.*
- *I let go and trust.*
- *I am an inspiration for others.*
- *I am an example of what is possible.*
- *Miracles are happening to me now.*
- *I am in flow with abundant health.*
- *It is safe for me to care for myself.*
- *I am aligned with positive healing energy.*

- *My strength and vitality increase daily.*
- *My healing is inspiring others.*
- *I know that abundant health is possible for me.*
- *I seek out examples of others who have healed.*
- *What I seek is seeking me.*
- *I have a loving relationship with my body.*
- *My body is in a constant state of loving renewal.*
- *I am young in spirit.*
- *I stand tall and free.*
- *I manifest perfect health now.*
- *I have so much fun in my life!*
- *All my desires are instantly met.*
- *I am strong and confident.*
- *All I need is within me now.*
- *I am kind to myself and love myself deeply and completely.*
- *I am unapologetic about making time for self-care.*
- *I love my life!*
- *I give myself permission to step into my healthy body.*
- *I am a healing machine!*
- *I see myself with love and tenderness.*
- *I am alive with the joy of living.*
- *I am aligned with complete health and vitality.*
- *I am always guided to my highest good.*
- *As my health grows, so does my contribution to the world.*
- *I have what it takes to be strong and healthy.*
- *I am kind to myself and love myself completely.*
- *I accept my own power.*
- *I am a powerful woman/man.*
- *I give and receive in equal measure.*
- *I am surrounded by love.*
- *I am restored to health, harmony, and peace.*

How to Use Affirmations

Now, it's time to choose your affirmations. You can select affirmations from the list I shared or write your own using the guidelines. In the beginning, you may want to just choose three to five affirmations and add more or different ones later.

Next, write down your affirmations. I like to write each affirmation on an index card. You can also write them in your journal or on your computer. I also like to keep affirmations in a note on my phone so I always have them with me.

Once you have the affirmations written down, read them out loud. The real power lies in the feelings you feel while reading the affirmations. Visualize yourself as the affirmation describes with as much detail as possible. Feel the feelings you'll experience when you achieve that affirmation.

Summary of Healing Habit #3: Manage Your Mind

- Choose your affirmations.
- Write your affirmations down.
- Recite your affirmations out loud, while feeling the feelings of achieving them. You could also record yourself reading your affirmations and listen to your own voice speaking your affirmations.

To implement Healing Habit #3, read (or listen to) your affirmations three times every day, morning, midday, and prior to bed. Now that you have established Healing Habits #1 and #2, you can do your affirmations immediately following these. If you record yourself reading the affirmations, you could listen to them as you're falling asleep when your mind is most suggestible. On your Healing Habit Tracker, add this habit to the daily practices and check off the box every time you practice the habit.

You can also manage your mind throughout the day, especially if you are experiencing pain. Rather than generating fear about the pain, you can manage your mind to help break the pain-fear cycle. When you notice the pain, you can use the affirmation "I am safe. This is temporary." You could also simply notice the pain with curiosity, saying, "I am curious about what I'm experiencing right now." Switching to safety or curiosity rather than fear will give the brain new ways to experience pain, rewiring new networks and sending a message of calm to the nervous system so it can let go of the need to protect you with pain.

Over time, you may want to use different affirmations to match whatever goal you're currently focused on, or perhaps a challenge you're currently facing. For example, when I was experiencing anxiety prior to a musical performance, I created affirmations to help me stay calm: "I have practiced and I am ready," "I am excited to share the gift of music with the audience," and so on.

Once you get in the habit of reprogramming your mind with affirmations, you'll find yourself more quickly switching to supportive self-talk that will shift your nervous system to a more relaxed state.

Healing Habit #4: Generate Love

Love is the ultimate healing emotion. Most of us have experienced a feeling of love at some point in our lives and can appreciate that it feels good in our bodies. Our goal in this Healing Habit is to experience feelings of love in your life every day to help regulate the nervous system and bathe every cell in your body in a healing vibration.

The Essence of Love

What is love? Love is a feeling, a vibration in the body. We often think of love as coming from outside of us, but this love is simply a reflection of the love that we feel inside. Rather than coming from outside of us, experiencing love is a process of removing the barriers to reveal the love that is already inside of you. It's who you *are*. Love is your true essence. As Rumi, the 13th-century mystic and poet, wrote, "Your task is not to seek for love, but merely to seek and find all the barriers within yourself that you have built against it."

While the concept that you are love may be hard to grasp, it may be easier if you are a parent and can recall seeing your baby (this could be a fur baby!) for the first time. When I first gazed upon each of my babies, it truly was love at first sight. In my eyes, they were perfect in every way, and I loved them unconditionally. It is that feeling we want to feel when we practice this Healing Habit.

The word love is also a verb. Considering love as an action word, we can intentionally take action to remove the barriers to love by generating a feeling of love and embracing self-love as a cornerstone for emotional and physical healing.

The Science of Love

Numerous studies have explored the science of love, revealing just how powerful love is for our emotional and physical well-being. Love is a powerful feeling, but it's not just a feeling. Love creates a cascade of biochemical and physiological processes that promote health and healing. For example, when we experience feelings of love, the body releases oxytocin, often called the "love hormone." Not only does oxytocin foster feelings of connection and bonding, but it also reduces stress, lowers inflammation, and strengthens the immune system.

Love is the catalyst to regulate the nervous system, by activating the parasympathetic or relaxation response, counteracting stress. In this state, blood pressure is lowered, all systems of the body work more efficiently, and the body can heal. Love is a powerful regulator of the nervous system.

Feelings of love and compassion create harmony and resonance within the body. Heart resonance refers to the harmonious vibration of the heart when we experience positive emotions, including love and compassion. The Heart-Math Institute has studied how stress and different emotional states affect the autonomic nervous system, hormones, immune response, heart, and brain. Their research has found that the most important measure of the relationship between psychological and physiological responses is heart-rate variability (HRV). HRV is a measure of harmony. High HRV is associated with being peaceful, calm, and overall better health. HRV increases when we take long, slow, deep breaths combined with positive emotions, called heart-focused or heart-resonance breathing. This allows for a variation in successive heartbeats and puts the heart and brain in a state of harmony. In this state, all body systems work better, improving health and relationships. With practice, self-awareness, and self-regulation, you can create a habit of generating love to increase HRV and induce heart harmony.

The ripple effect of love extends beyond individual well-being. Vibrations from the heart are the strongest vibrations in the body, currently measurable from several feet beyond the physical body. When we cultivate love and compassion within ourselves, this vibration radiates outward, affecting those around us. You may have experienced this feeling when you are around a person you love or have been in the presence of a spiritually evolved person. Love creates a positive feedback loop, contributing to a more loving and compassionate world. Your generating feelings of love can inspire love in others, creating a positive movement toward greater emotional resilience.

Cultivating Love

Cultivating love requires intentionality and practice, which is why this is one of your Healing Habits. This Healing Habit is about setting aside a few minutes each day for heart-resonance breathing. You can follow this as a guideline or go to http://painfreeonpurpose.com/ or use the QR Code provided on page 158 to download an audio version.

Find a quiet space, sit comfortably, gently close your eyes, and focus on your breath. Inhale deeply through your nose, allowing your abdomen to expand, and then exhale slowly through your mouth. If it feels right for you, touch one or both hands to the heart area of your chest. Imagine that, as you inhale, the breath fills your heart, expanding your heart with each inhale. Next, bring to mind a person, place, or event that makes you feel happy, joyful, compassionate, peaceful, or any other positive emotion. In your mind, make this memory rich in detail, noticing what you see, hear, and feel. Notice the feeling you have in your heart. Now, completely focus on this feeling in your heart and imagine it getting bigger with each inhale. Imagine it doubling in size, and then getting so big it fills your entire body, then outside your body, and then filling the room you are in. Breathe with this feeling for a few moments. Next, imagine pulling this loving feeling back into your heart, knowing that it's always there and that you can expand it any time you want to.

Summary of Healing Habit #4: Generate Love

- Get into a comfortable position and relax your body. Set a timer for three minutes, or longer.
- Close your eyes and focus on the breath.
- Do heart-resonance breathing by imagining breathing into the heart area, then recalling a memory that helps you feel love, notice the feeling in your heart, and let the feeling expand beyond your body.
- When the timer ends, gently bring the expanding feeling back into your heart, tucking it in for later.

To implement Healing Habit #4, practice heart-resonance breathing three times every day, morning, midday, and prior to bed. You can tie this new habit in with the other habits you've now established. Once you've created calm with breathwork, you can shift to generating love, seamlessly merging Healing Habits #1 and #4 together. On your Healing Habit Tracker or other tracking system, add this habit to the daily practices and check off a box every time you practice the habit.

Of course, you can feel love at any time throughout the day. With increased awareness, you'll notice when you're not experiencing that loving feeling and can intentionally and quickly shift to feeling love whenever you choose to ... and why not choose to do that most of the time?

Milestones for Step 2: Explore

- Healing Habit #3: Manage Your Mind each morning, midday, and prior to bed.
- Healing Habit #4: Generate Love each morning, midday, and prior to bed.

You can implement these habits simultaneously or begin with Healing Habit #3 until it becomes automatic, then add Healing Habit #4. Do what works best and is easiest for you.

This step of the DESIGN Blueprint is complete when you are practicing each of these habits daily with consistency until each becomes automatic for you, or for at least 28 days. If you find any of your established habits slipping as you add a new habit, then go back to the daily practice of the earlier habits until they are firmly established, and then reintroduce the new habit.

Once Healing Habits #3 and #4 are firmly established as part of your daily routine, you're ready to move on to Step 3, Surrender. Don't forget to celebrate achieving the milestones for the Explore step! Treat yourself in some way to reward yourself (and your brain) for the wonderful progress you're making. Well done, my friend!

Chapter 7

Step 3: Surrender

"And I said to my body softly, 'I want to be your friend.' It took a long breath and replied, 'I have been waiting my whole life for this."
—Nayyirah Waheed

The Surrender step is about letting go of the protection you've built up and trusting that your body and your life have been supporting you all along. You'll surrender to your body's need for deep restorative sleep, and you'll learn to accept that all of life is happening for you, for your growth and development. The two Healing Habits for the Surrender step are:

- Healing Habit #5: Sleep and Rest
- Healing Habit #6: Forgive and Release

Let's learn about these habits to help you surrender to support your nervous system and help your body heal.

Healing Habit #5: Sleep and Rest

Sleep is a precious cornerstone of your well-being, especially when you're navigating life with chronic pain. The problem I had, like many people with chronic pain, was that pain interrupted my sleep. I also realized later that my dysregulated nervous system was contributing to sleep problems because my body wasn't making the right hormones at the right time. A body that's not getting deep, restorative sleep simply cannot heal.

What happens while we sleep? Despite the stillness of the body, the brain remains incredibly active during sleep, orchestrating crucial processes that impact every facet of health. In those silent hours of slumber, your body tirelessly supports brain function and nurtures physical health. Sleep isn't just a matter of feeling refreshed the next morning; it profoundly influences your ability to heal and manage chronic pain.

Think of sleep as the conductor of an orchestra, harmonizing the intricate rhythms of your body's systems. Not just a biological necessity, but a profound interconnection of mind, body, and spirit. Recognizing the impact of sleep on every aspect of your health, creating sleep-supportive habits will help make every night's rest bring you closer to a brighter tomorrow.

Knowing that the body heals during sleep was a huge motivator for me and helped me make sleep a priority. I was willing to do whatever I could to improve my sleep. Instead of staying up late, trying to "get things done," I surrendered to sleep. I dove into the research to learn about what's going on while we sleep and how to let my body get deep, restorative sleep.

Understanding the Hormonal Dance of Sleep

Our bodies engage in a beautiful dance orchestrated by a trio of hormones: serotonin, cortisol, and melatonin. These hormones ebb and flow throughout the day with our circadian rhythms, exerting profound effects on our sleep-wake cycles. While light exposure plays a significant role in regulating these hormones, various lifestyle factors and behaviors also influence their balance. Understanding the intricate interplay of these hormones is essential for fostering restorative sleep.

Serotonin, often referred to as the "feel-good" neurotransmitter, plays a crucial role in regulating sleep. Its levels should peak during the daytime to facilitate the production of melatonin, the hormone responsible for inducing sleep. Exposure to natural sunlight is instrumental in boosting serotonin production. Morning sunlight exposure is particularly beneficial for setting up sleep-supporting production of serotonin. Beyond sunlight, activities that promote relaxation and well-being, like mindfulness meditation, spending time in nature, and engaging in hobbies, can also enhance serotonin levels, contributing to better sleep quality.

While cortisol is often dubbed "the stress hormone," it serves essential functions in our bodies, including regulating our sleep-wake cycles. Naturally tied to the light-dark cycles, cortisol levels should be highest in the mornings, gradually tapering off as the day progresses. Insufficient exposure to natural light can disrupt cortisol rhythms, impacting our ability to fall asleep and stay asleep. Morning sunlight exposure not only aids in cortisol production but also primes our bodies for physical activity, as cortisol levels increase with exercise. Because of this, morning movement can further support healthy cortisol levels and promote better sleep quality.

As the primary sleep regulator, melatonin's production operates in opposition to cortisol. When cortisol levels are elevated, melatonin levels are suppressed, and vice versa. As the day transitions into night, cortisol levels should naturally decline, and melatonin production should increase, telling the mind and body to prepare for sleep. Since serotonin governs the synthesis of melatonin, enhancing serotonin production during the day with the strategies mentioned earlier can lead to improved sleep quality.

Achieving a delicate balance between these hormones is pivotal in optimizing sleep quality. By understanding the intricate interplay of serotonin, cortisol, and melatonin, and the influence of light exposure, participating in restful activities and physical activity, we can empower ourselves to cultivate healthier sleep habits. From prioritizing morning sunlight exposure to engaging in regular exercise and mindfulness practices, every choice we make throughout the day contributes to supporting our best sleep.

We Need Routines

We are creatures of rhythm. Some obvious rhythms are our pulsing heart, breathing, menstrual cycles, and digestion. Other not-so-obvious routines are going on within our bodies, like the release of hormones and neurotransmitters like cortisol, melatonin, and serotonin.

These biorhythms, or circadian rhythms, are critical to our health and well-being and have a major impact on our sleep as well. Many of our biorhythms are controlled by a trio of organs: the hypothalamus and the pituitary gland in the brain, and the adrenal glands, two walnut-sized glands, which sit on top of the kidneys. The hypothalamus, pituitary gland, and adrenals are often collectively referred to as the HPA axis. These three work together to regulate the secretion of cortisol.

The hypothalamus houses the master controller of our biorhythms. The biggest influencer affecting the hypothalamus and circadian clocks is the light-dark cycle. Our body detects when it is light during the day and dark during the night. Other factors affecting our circadian clocks are exposure to bright lights, meal timing, physical exercise, stress, and sleep routines.

While we can't regulate when the sun rises and sets, many other factors mentioned above *are* within our control. We can control the timing of when we are exposed to natural and artificial light. We can control the timing of meals, physical exercise, and sleep routines. By creating routines for these activities, we can assist the HPA axis in doing the job it was meant to do. When the HPA axis is functioning well, optimal sleep is achievable. Routines can be our superpower and can help us get better sleep.

Let's consider morning, midday, and evening routines to support better sleep and help you on your healing path.

Morning Habits for Better Sleep

From the previous discussion, we can see that getting better sleep at night begins in the morning by naturally increasing serotonin and cortisol early in the day. Exposure of your retinas to natural light by getting outdoors as soon as possible in the mornings, within the first thirty minutes of waking, if possible, helps establish proper serotonin production. While this may be more challenging in the winter months, sticking to a regular morning routine, even if you can't get outdoors, will help keep the dance of hormones in balance.

Take Restorative Breaks During the Day

Cortisol should taper off as the day progresses to support natural melatonin production. To help prevent elevated afternoon cortisol, take short, restorative breaks throughout the day. This is especially important if you are experiencing cognitive or emotional strain. Even a few minutes at midday can significantly reduce afternoon cortisol levels, helping to improve sleep at night. Your break could simply be taking a few minutes for slow, conscious breathing, journaling, walking in nature, or engaging in another activity that feels calming for you. Of course, anytime you notice you are feeling stressed during the day, take a break to restore calm.

Evening Sleep Hygiene

If you're a parent, you probably know that children sleep better when they have a wind-down routine before bed. When my children were little, we had a bedtime routine for them. We knew that they needed to have quiet time before bed so they would fall asleep more easily and stay asleep all night. As adults, we may think we don't need a bedtime routine, but the truth is that we still do.

Critical to our sleep quality, as children and adults, is what we do in the last one to two hours *before* going to bed. This is when we want to relax our minds and send a signal that it is time for sleep.

Here are six things you can do to relax your brain before bedtime:

- **Lessen the Light.** In the evenings, dim the lights in your home to simulate the sun going down. Avoid exposing your eyes to blue light from television or electronic devices for at least one hour before bedtime. Blue light, especially, inhibits the production of melatonin, which is needed for optimal sleep.

- **Avoid Eating and Drinking.** If our body is busy digesting food, it's more difficult to settle down for sleep. Drinking during the evening can result in a bladder that needs to be emptied during the night, disrupting sleep. Alcohol, while it may help you fall asleep, disrupts sleep cycles during the night.

- **Send a Sleep Message.** For the last hour before bed, do something relaxing, rather than stimulating. Read, journal, listen to calming music, do light stretching, meditate, have a bath, or do any activity that you find relaxing. Especially avoid exposure to news. In this way, you are telling your brain it is time to sleep.

- **Empty Your Mind.** Write down things that are on your mind. The very act of dumping from your brain to paper can relieve built-up tension or stress.

- **Breathe Deeply.** Taking several long, deep breaths into the belly helps oxygenate the brain and calms the nervous system. Focusing your attention on the breath can also help take your mind off other things.

- **Feel Gratitude.** After you turn off your light, close your eyes and think of at least three things that happened during the day which you can be grateful for. Feelings of gratitude send a signal to your brain that all is well, allowing you to sleep more peacefully.

You'll also want to ensure your bedroom is conducive to sleepy slumber. Your bedroom should be quiet, free of electronics, dark, and at the right temperature, so as not to wake you up. Ideally, your bedroom should be a place for sleep and not where you watch screens or work.

Putting It All Together

When you think about it, not sleeping is a form of protection, just like pain. If our nervous system is on high alert for "danger," the last thing it thinks we need is sleep. We need to help our brain and nervous system understand that it is safe to shift to the parasympathetic, rest-and-digest state and surrender to sleep. We can help do that with the choices we make throughout the day.

When I began consciously making the choices to support better sleep at night, my sleep improved, and that helped my nervous system relax and let go of trying to protect me. I started keeping a regular waking and sleeping routine, even on the weekends. My morning routine became sacrosanct—and it still is. Exposing my retinas to natural light in the morning became part of my morning routine. When I learned about the power of a midday break, I added that in, too. In the evening, just like I did with my kids when they were little, I created a wind-down routine before bed. Because I live so far east, it means online events hosted in North America are often late into my evening, so I got some blue-light blocking glasses for those times when I couldn't avoid looking at a screen at night. All these combined to help me have more restful slumbers ... and helped support my body's natural ability to heal.

Let's put these together as a Healing Habit to support you in getting deep, restorative sleep, too.

Summary of Healing Habit #5: Sleep and Rest

- Morning Routine: Set a regular wake-up time and get outside for several minutes within thirty minutes of waking.
- Midday Break: Choose a time to take a break for 10–30 minutes each day and set reminders to make it happen. Decide what restorative activity you will do for the break.

- Evening Routine: Set a regular bedtime and begin a wind-down routine for sixty minutes prior to going to bed, where you don't look at any screens, lights are dim, and you do something relaxing for you.

Now that you've established the first four Healing Habits, you will find it easier to add Sleep and Rest. You'll set an alarm for a regular waking time (even on the weekends), do your Healing Habits 1, 2, 3, and 4, then step outside for a few minutes to let the morning light enter your eyes. When the weather is warm, you could do your morning Healing Habits 1, 2, 3, and 4 while outdoors so that your retinas are exposed to morning light. Your midday break time can be when you practice Healing Habits 1, 2, 3, and 4. Similarly, your evening routine can be when you practice Healing Habits 1, 2, 3, and 4. Do whatever works best for you. The key is establishing a routine. On your Healing Habit Tracker, add this habit to the daily practices and check off every time you practice these habits.

Healing Habit #6: Forgive and Release

As Byron Katie wisely said, "Forgiveness is just another name for freedom." Forgiveness doesn't mean letting someone off the hook for wronging you, but it is a way to free yourself from the negative energies that bind you to them. If you lack forgiveness, the situation or person is hurting no one but you.

Therefore, the act of forgiveness isn't something you do for another person, but a gift you give yourself. Forgiveness is a practice that can set you free, not just emotionally but physically as well. When we hang onto resentments, hurt, and blame, we block the flow of abundance in our lives, including health abundance. Negative emotions associated with events and people that hurt us can literally get "stuck" in our bodies, causing physical pain or illness.

Emotions are felt as feelings vibrating at different frequencies in the body. All cells respond to frequencies, which might sound strange; however, science has proven this to be true. Cells are made up of atoms, which, as revealed by quantum physics, are made of 99.9% energy. This explains why cells are sensitive to vibrational frequencies, like emotions, sounds, and electromagnetic frequencies, which are all forms of energy. In her book *You Can Heal Your Life*, Louise Hay lists many illnesses and physical problems along with the associated emotions. Resentment, guilt, shame, fear, and anger are common emotions associated with pain. These emotions are part and parcel with a lack of forgiveness. Resentment, grudges, and other negative feelings associated with unforgiving keep the nervous system in a stressed state, maintaining the protection of pain and making it impossible to heal. To heal your physical pain, you must release the emotional pain. Forgiveness can be the greatest gift you give yourself.

Why Forgiveness Is Hard

We know that a lack of forgiveness is not good for us. Why then is it so hard to forgive? When someone wrongs us, it hurts, and we tend to want to nurse those hurts and feel righteous in our hurt. We rehearse that hurt over and over again, holding onto the resentment tightly. Even if we don't keep rehearsing, we may be harboring old hurts that we are not even aware of in our subconscious mind. You may even find that the person you most need to forgive is yourself, for things you did or didn't do.

Often, when we hang on to resentments, we repeat the incidents over and over, cementing our own point of view in our minds. This makes it difficult to see the situation from another perspective. But there is always another perspective, another story. We may never know the whole story, but we can let go of past hurts by appreciating that *all* our life experiences have led us to exactly where we are today.

Perhaps the thing you can't forgive is the pain, or the situation that caused the pain. Resentment, hurt, or anger you feel about this is very likely perpetuating the pain cycle, and having the exact opposite effect you want. I remember feeling very angry and that, despite living a healthy life and being active, my body had "betrayed" me with pain. Viewing pain in a new light, that this pain was happening *for* me, not *to* me, allowed me to see my life differently and forgive the past, and helped to eventually let go of pain.

You may feel that you are not quite ready to fully forgive someone or a situation, or you thought you'd forgiven them but now find you haven't quite got there yet. Allow space for that, too. If this is the case, try a smaller step by practicing empathy. Try seeing the situation from the other person's point of view. Can you see that they did the best they could with their set of life experiences and what they knew, and you would do the exact same thing if you had their experiences and circumstances? This may help you release the heaviness and feel lighter.

Practicing Forgiveness

The first step of forgiveness is to decide that you no longer want to carry around resentments. I hope from the previous discussion you understand that harboring resentments will block you from healing and will perpetuate pain.

The second step is to commit to practicing forgiveness. Forgiveness is rarely a one-and-done type of thing. There can be many layers of forgiveness, and simply day-to-day living can build up grievances and resentments. Mindset mentor Mary Morrisey says we need to practice regular forgiveness to wash away resentments that build up from everyday living.

There are many books written on forgiveness, and there are some beautiful practices, such as the ancient Hawaiian forgiveness technique of Ho'oponopono and the Buddhist Loving Kindness meditation. Other techniques include finding empathy for the person who has hurt you, practicing acceptance that all your experiences are happening for you, not to you, writing a letter to the person and then burning it, practicing a forgiveness meditation, or working with a qualified forgiveness therapist.

When I looked back on my life, I realized I was holding on to resentments against people who had hurt me. There were incidents and memories that activated strong feelings in me when I thought about them. These feelings were a sure indicator that I had forgiveness work to do, so I could fully heal. Forgiveness was not a one-and-done process for me. I had to come back many times and with different techniques. I do believe now that all those experiences were opportunities for me to learn and grow, no matter when I decided to forgive. Perhaps on some level, my soul came here to have those experiences so that I could learn forgiveness. From this viewpoint, I could accept that these experiences were gifts, even if they were in strange packaging! Practicing empathy was very helpful for me, too. I imagined the person who hurt me as the child version of themselves, remembering that "hurt people hurt people." This helped me understand that their behavior wasn't really about me, that I just happened to be the one in the line of fire. Eventually, I could think of these people and events without resentment, without the emotional charge, and that's when I knew I had truly forgiven.

The Healing Habit of Forgive and Release will help cleanse your perceptions, emotions, and ways of seeing things, so you can experience life without the drag of unresolved ideas about what's in your history and what's in your journey. Here, I'm sharing a simple forgiveness exercise using journaling prompts. Feel free to substitute another forgiveness practice or try different practices. The important thing is to forgive and release until you no longer feel an emotional charge about past and current events and people in your life. Remember that this is a many-layered process.

Summary of Healing Habit #6: Forgive and Release

- Choose a person or situation that you will forgive (this could be you).
- List three things you have gained from this relationship or situation.
- Journal about not knowing the whole story.
- Practice empathy by seeing the situation from the perspective of the other person, or yourself at that stage of life, remembering that people have done the best they could, based on their set of life experiences.

Unlike the Healing Habits we've established so far, Forgive and Release is a habit you will do once a week or whenever you notice you are harboring resentments. I like to set aside time on Sundays for weekly reflection, which I call the Weekly Review and Preview. Choose any day that works for you, but schedule the time on your calendar to help ensure it happens. Throughout the week, notice when you have thoughts around irritation, resentment, hurt, or anger. Make a note of these and set aside time in your weekly reflection to practice forgiveness. Of course, you can practice forgiveness in the moment, and over time, you will find it easier to do this.

Milestones for Step 3: Surrender

- Healing Habit #5: Practice Sleep and Rest habits each morning, midday, and evening.
- Healing Habit #6: Practice Forgive and Release weekly or as needed.

You can work on implementing Healing Habits #5 and #6 together, or start with Healing Habit #5 until it becomes automatic, then bring in Healing Habit #6 on a weekly basis.

This step in the DESIGN Blueprint is complete when you have incorporated both of these habits with consistency until each becomes automatic for you, or for at least 28 days. Once you are doing that, you're ready for the next step. But, before you move on to Integrate, celebrate the Surrender step. Reward yourself in some way for making these new habits part of your life to support you in your healing. I'm celebrating you, too. Good for you, my friend!

Chapter 8

Step 4: Integrate

"Take care of your body. It's the only place you have to live."
—Jim Rohn

The Integrate step is where we merge together mind, body, and spirit for holistic healing. We'll focus on supporting the body by helping it absorb nutrients and live more naturally. By helping the body receive the nutrients it needs for new cell creation and reducing exposure to toxins, we are helping to create the environment in which the body can heal and let go of pain.

The two Healing Habits for the Integrate step are:

- Healing Habit #7: Nourish Thyself
- Healing Habit #8: Embrace Natural Living

Let's learn about these habits to help you support your physical body.

Healing Habit #7: Nourish Thyself

I'm all for eating healthy foods. The food we eat becomes the building blocks for all our cells, so of course, we should eat quality food. However, we could eat great food, but if we aren't digesting and absorbing it efficiently, then the body won't receive the nutrients it needs. Along my healing journey, I rushed too quickly into using food as medicine. I began an elimination diet, cutting out food groups like gluten, dairy, and sugar. This certainly did help lower inflammation initially, but it was also very stressful. Eventually, I developed orthorexia, an obsession with healthy eating. This fear of food created a lot of stress for me, and, I believe, in the long run, slowed down my healing. When we are stressed about food, we don't digest well, and therefore, we won't absorb the nutrients of the foods we are eating.

For this reason, Healing Habit #7 begins with mindful eating. This will support the digestive process by helping the nervous system know that it's safe to focus on digestion, rather than protection.

Digestion begins in the brain. The brain sends signals to the body, preparing the digestive system to work effectively. The practices of this Healing Habit help keep the autonomic nervous system in the parasympathetic, rest-and-digest state while eating. Your thoughts matter—*especially* while eating. That's why it's so important to practice eating mindfully.

For many years, I was busy being busy. I had an active family, and that meant eating on the run sometimes. Still, we tried to mostly sit down together as a family for suppers, and those are times I treasure. However, our hectic lifestyle meant that we got into the habit of eating quickly, even when we did sit down for meals. I remember noticing that when we had guests for supper, often we would be finished eating while our guests were only halfway through their plate of food. At the time, I was a little amused by how fast we ate but didn't think much more of it. Yes, I knew that the general advice was to eat slowly, but I didn't have time for that!

Fast-forward to 2016 when autoimmune disease entered my life. I had no idea that poor digestion could lead to inflammation. It turns out that rushing through meals can be harmful to your health. Believe it or not, eating too quickly for so many years was a contributor to my autoimmune disease because poor digestion began to trigger my immune system.

What I learned is that *how* you eat can be as important as *what* you eat.

Eating mindfully means paying attention to the process of eating without judgment and trusting your body's natural hunger and fullness cues. It's a healthy way to reconnect with food, listen to your body, and help your digestive system with its task of breaking down food to fuel you.

As Thich Nhat Hanh, global spiritual leader and peace activist, said, "Mindful eating allows us to fully appreciate the sensory delight of eating and to be more conscious of the amount and nature of all that we eat and drink." Eating should be a delightful, sensory process, and it can be so when we practice mindful eating.

Some Tips for Eating Mindfully

Eating mindfully is about cultivating a practice of awareness while eating. To help you stay in the present moment while eating, consider these three aspects of mindful eating: relax, savor, and chew.

Relax:

- Sit down to eat at a table set beautifully, perhaps with candles and flowers
- Turn off distractions such as the TV or devices
- Take three slow breaths before you begin eating
- Feel gratitude for the food you are about to eat

Savor:

- Take a few moments to notice the colors, aromas, texture, and taste of your food as you eat
- Be in the moment, rather than letting your mind wander
- If you live with other people, eat, talk, and laugh together
- Notice the fullness in your belly and stop eating before you are full

Chew:

- Put only amounts that you can chew easily in your mouth at a time
- Chew food thoroughly until it is nearly a paste
- Slow down by putting utensils down between bites

- Take a full, deep breath before picking utensils up again

Becoming a mindful eater can take a lifetime of practice, especially for those of us who are used to rushing. As a starting point for this Healing Habit, find three objects to remind you to *relax, savor,* and *chew* while you eat. Put these objects in the place where you eat most of your meals, and then simply practice mindful eating at every meal. My three objects are a candle to remind me to relax, a little vase of roses to remind me to savor ("stop and smell the roses"), and a wooden carving of a Buddha with his hands in his lap to remind me to do the same thing as a chew. These objects are on the kitchen island where my husband and I eat most of our meals.

Mindful Snacking

What about between meals, when you aren't sitting down to eat? We often eat between meals even if we aren't truly hungry. Unless we really need food, it's easier on the digestive system if we aren't continuously giving it work to do. The immune system will also get a break. About 80% of our immune system resides in the gut, so every time we eat, we are challenging it, like an overworked police force.

Before you get something from the refrigerator or pantry, remember to "HALT." The word HALT is an acronym to remind you to stop before you snack and notice if you are snacking because you're hungry or if there is an emotional reason. If you find yourself reaching for a snack, stop and ask yourself:

- H: Am I hungry? Then, eat, but choose something healthy.
- A: Am I angry? If so, do a physical activity that matches the level of emotion you feel.
- L: Am I lonely (or bored)? Call a friend or do something kind for another person.
- T: Am I thirsty? Or tired? If you're thirsty, drink water. If you're tired, just go to bed.

To remind yourself to HALT, write the word "HALT" on Post-It notes and stick them to the outside or inside the refrigerator or pantry. These will get your attention and help you HALT when you reach for a snack.

As you become a more conscious eater, eventually, when you cycle through the DESIGN Blueprint again, you can go further by nourishing yourself with healthier food choices. Meal planning is a great way to start because when we plan meals, we generally make better choices and are more likely to stick with them. You may want to experiment with fasting practices to support your body. But for now, you will nourish yourself by practicing mindful eating.

Summary of Healing Habit #7: Nourish Thyself

- Find three objects to remind you to relax, savor, and chew while eating.
- Place these objects where you eat most meals.
- Practice mindful eating daily, relaxing while you eat, savoring the aromas and flavors, and thoroughly chewing your food.
- Write the word "HALT" on Post-It notes and place them where you typically go for snacks between meals.
- Practice mindful snacking by HALTing to ask yourself if there is an emotion behind your urge to eat.

Healing Habit #7 is a new habit you'll do with something you are already doing, eating. Your cue will be the reminder objects and HALT notes you'll have in your eating areas. Mindful eating is a lifetime practice. There are going to be days when you are rushed and you're going to forget to eat mindfully. The goal is to create awareness and cultivate a habit of eating mindfully most of the time. Rather than being a habit to check off on the Healing Habit Tracker, mindful eating is about creating a new state of being while eating. Your digestive system and your body will thank you.

Healing Habit #8: Embrace Natural Living

This habit is a big one and likely one you will be working on throughout your life. For the first time around the DESIGN Blueprint, we'll focus on micro steps. Embracing natural living doesn't mean you have to live in a cave. Rather, it's about helping the body build resilience, so you have more capacity for healing. We'll focus on taking micro steps in three areas: connecting with nature, reducing chemical exposure through personal care products, and reducing toxins in the food we eat. This will help lower the toxic load so that the body has more energy for healing.

It should come as no surprise that the amount of toxins surrounding us daily is growing. Humans once lived close to the earth. However, modern comforts, conveniences, and urban living have distanced us from the natural environment. In many ways, this disconnection has been detrimental to health. Through the Industrial Revolution, we were introduced to synthetic substances and environmental stressors, impacting both the Earth and our health. Now, we have increased exposure to chemicals and electromagnetic frequencies (EMFs) compared to previous generations. Dealing with environmental stressors requires a lot of energy from our bodies, and that means less energy is available for healing.

Numerous studies have shown that connecting with nature reduces stress, boosts immune function, and enhances creativity. In this habit of embracing natural living, you'll consciously appreciate your natural surroundings when outdoors and connect your bare feet to the earth, a practice called grounding or earthing. Studies have shown that health benefits include reduced inflammation, improved sleep, and enhanced well-being. If you live in a colder climate like I do, touching bare feet to the earth may not be practical during the winter months. In that case, do what you can, and explore other ways to ground, like grounding sheets or mats.

You'll also focus on reducing exposure to toxins through your skin by gradually replacing personal care products with more natural and organic ones. Read ingredient labels or research ingredients and choose ones that don't contain parabens, phthalates, and chemical fragrance. These ingredients are known hormone disrupters and carcinogens. Gradually, on a weekly basis, decide on one personal care product you can replace with a more natural one to support your body by not making it work so hard.

Likewise, let's clean up what we put in our bodies through what we eat and drink. A starting point is the containers we store our food in. Food will absorb chemicals from plastic containers, and those chemicals eventually end up in our bodies. Gradually, replace plastic food storage containers and drinking vessels with glass equivalents. Choose at least one item each week until you've eliminated all plastic. Eventually, you can consider what you cook your food in and the utensils you use while cooking, and the food itself, choosing more fresh and organic foods.

Summary of Healing Habit #8: Embrace Natural Living

- Connect with nature daily by getting outside and appreciating your surroundings, ideally grounding by connecting bare feet to the earth.
- Each week, replace one personal care product with a less toxic one, free of parabens, phthalates, and chemical fragrance.
- Each week, replace one plastic food storage container with a glass equivalent.

Since you've already established Healing Habit #5 and are going outside in the mornings, you can add in appreciating nature and grounding at the same time. On your Healing Habit Tracker, add "Connect with Nature" to your morning daily habits. The other parts of Healing Habit #8 are weekly practices I include in my Weekly Review and Preview. As part of your weekly review practice, you can consider which personal care products and food storage containers you will replace next and when you will do that. Put these commitments on your calendar and check them off once you've replaced them.

Milestones for Step 4: Integrate

- Healing Habit #7: Practice Nourish Thyself at mealtimes by eating mindfully.
- Healing Habit #8: Embrace Natural Living on a daily and weekly basis.

You can work on implementing these habits simultaneously or start with Healing Habit #7 until it becomes automatic, then integrate Healing Habit #8.

The Integrate step is complete when you have incorporated each of these habits with consistency until each becomes automatic for you, or for at least 28 days, remembering that these are also a lifetime practice so the habit is cultivating awareness. Once you are doing that, you're ready to move on to Step 5, Generate. Before moving on, make sure you reward yourself for integrating these new habits into your life. Celebrate how far you've come and the progress you're making!

Chapter 9

Step 5: Generate

"There is a vitality, a life force, an energy, a quickening, that is translated through you into action, and because there is only one of you in all time, this expression is unique."
—Martha Graham

Step 5, Generate, is about activating intelligent energy and vitality. In this step, you will discover the art of actively generating a new version of yourself by elevating your vibrational energy on physical, mental, and emotional levels, propelling yourself toward healing.

The two Healing Habits for the Generate step are:

- Healing Habit #9: Find Your Friends
- Healing Habit #10: Move with Joy

Let's learn how we can build habits to generate intelligent energy to support the body's natural healing ability.

Healing Habit #9: Find Your Friends

Relationships are the cornerstone of our human experience, impacting not only our emotional health but our physical health as well. This Healing Habit is about the transformative power of nurturing meaningful relationships, emphasizing the importance of building connections and cultivating a sense of belonging and support. It's also about releasing, or taking a break from, those relationships that are not supporting your healing journey. Let's explore how the quality of our relationships significantly impacts the body's ability to heal and how you can create a Healing Habit of cultivating supportive relationships.

Be Your Own Best Friend

The foundation of all healthy relationships begins with the relationship we have with ourselves. Self-compassion and self-care are vital. When we treat ourselves with kindness and respect, we set a standard for how we expect to be treated by others. Monitor your self-talk. Would you speak to a dear friend the way you speak to yourself? A mind and body that continue to receive loving messages can heal. The opposite is also true; if we continually have negative self-talk, the message sent to every cell in the body is that they are not wanted or loved. Practical exercises such as daily affirmations, mindfulness meditation, and self-reflective journaling can enhance your relationship with yourself. When you notice negative self-talk, remind yourself to stop. You can even say out loud or silently, "Stop. We don't do that anymore." Remember that you are in charge of your thoughts, and you get to choose what thoughts you think. By being your own best friend, you reduce stress and cultivate an inner resilience that positively influences your external relationships.

When my mother passed, I felt like I had lost my best friend. She was the one who always spoke to me lovingly, who was my biggest cheerleader. Without her, I realized that I had to be my own champion. I needed to be the one who spoke kindly to me. This was a huge realization and a shift. For most of my life, I had a running narrative of negative self-talk. I never felt good enough. I knew this had to change for my body to heal. In the beginning, it was still my mother's voice I could hear in my mind: *Janey, I'm so proud of you. I love you. You are a kind person. You can do this.* Eventually, I noticed that it was *my* voice saying these things. In my morning journaling practice, I started a daily practice of writing a loving message to myself, and I included loving messages in my daily affirmations. Gradually, I could feel the shift and really feel the love within me, that I was *worthy* of love.

At the heart of self-love is a sense of worthiness. In the wise words of Brené Brown, "When you get to a place where you understand that love and belonging, your worthiness is a birthright and not something you have to earn, anything is possible." Your worthiness is non-negotiable. By the very act of being born, you are worthy. Your worthiness is never tarnished. You are amazing, and you can't take credit for it. Think back to when a baby (yours or someone else's) was born. Were they anything less than amazing? Could they take credit for it? Feelings of unworthiness stem from opinions, either your own or those of others. But since you are inherently worthy, your opinion of yourself doesn't diminish your worth, and neither does anyone else's opinion of you. No matter what you've done to others or yourself, it hasn't touched your worthiness. Your worthiness remains intact. There is nothing you can do or think that makes you any less worthy, and no one else can take that from you. Once you accept that you are inherently worthy, you will begin to love yourself and be able to receive love from others. Your nervous system will begin to relax, and your body can begin to release pain.

The Science of Connection

Let's next consider our relationships with other people. Scientific research consistently shows that strong social connections are crucial for maintaining good health and well-being. Studies have demonstrated that individuals with robust social networks tend to live longer, healthier lives. For instance, a landmark study in 2010 found that people with strong social relationships had a 50% improvement in mortality rates compared to those with weaker social ties (Holt-Lunstad et al., 2010). This effect was consistent across age, gender, initial health status, cause of death, and follow-up period. Another study in 2010 found consistent evidence linking a low quantity or quality of social ties with a host of conditions, including the development and progression of cardiovascular disease, atherosclerosis, autonomic dysregulation, high blood pressure, cancer and delayed cancer recovery, and slower wound healing (Umberson & Montez, 2010).

We are hardwired for belonging. The amygdala part of the brain links relationships with survival. If the amygdala feels a "threat" of not being accepted by the "tribe," it interprets this as a mortal danger. A constant felt sense of not belonging creates a continual stress response. As Lisa Olivera, author of *Already Enough,* said, "Just because no one else can heal or do your inner work for you doesn't mean you can, should, or need to do it alone."

Positive social interactions help reduce stress and regulate the nervous system, which can help lower pain. A supportive social circle can also promote healthy behaviors, which lead to improved immune function and reduced inflammation. When we feel connected and supported, our bodies produce lower levels of the stress hormone cortisol and higher levels of oxytocin, which promotes feelings of love and bonding. These biochemical responses play a crucial role in calming the nervous system and promoting healing. Having a strong social circle can help promote healing.

Assess Your Social Circle

Not all social interactions are supportive. Therefore, it's essential to honestly assess the quality of your current social circle. This involves a thoughtful evaluation of how you feel about your social, family, and intimate relationships. Questions to ask yourself include: Do your relationships uplift and support you? Do you feel drained or energized after spending time with certain individuals? Are there patterns of negativity or toxicity in any of your interactions? Tools like journaling or reflecting on recent social interactions can help identify supportive and non-supportive connections. By recognizing these patterns, you can make informed decisions about which relationships to nurture and which to reconsider.

Building Meaningful Connections

Having a chronic pain condition may mean that you've become isolated from friends and family members. You may have found it too physically demanding to socialize. Physical limitations may mean you haven't been able to participate in activities you used to enjoy and the people you enjoyed doing them with.

Prioritizing and maintaining connections requires deliberate effort. Schedule regular meetups, phone calls, or video chats with loved ones. Simple gestures like sending a thoughtful message or planning a small gathering can go a long way in nurturing relationships. The quality of time spent together is often more important than the quantity of time.

Meeting new people and expanding your social circle can bring fresh perspectives and enrich your life. Engage in activities that interest you, join clubs or groups, and participate in community events. Volunteering is also a great way to meet like-minded individuals while contributing to a cause you care about. By stepping out of your comfort zone, you open yourself up to new and potentially rewarding relationships.

Being part of a community provides a sense of belonging and support. Whether it's a neighborhood group, a religious community, or an online forum, engaging with a community can provide emotional and practical support. Look for communities that resonate with your values and interests. Being involved in a community not only benefits you but also allows you to contribute and make a positive impact on others.

Releasing Non-Supportive Relationships

Not all relationships are beneficial, and it's important to recognize when a relationship is not serving you. Toxic or draining relationships can significantly impact our health, causing emotional turmoil and activating the stress response of the nervous system.

Recognizing toxic relationships is the first step towards emotional freedom. These are relationships that consistently cause stress, anxiety, or negativity. It's important to understand that ending or distancing from such relationships is a form of self-care. Strategies for gracefully ending a relationship include honest conversations about your feelings, setting firm boundaries, and gradually reducing contact. Approach this process with compassion for yourself and the other person involved, using empathy and forgiveness practices you learned in the previous chapter.

A question that often comes up is around people whom you simply can't remove from your life, such as close family members. In these situations, scaling back interactions, even temporarily, may help you gain perspective. You can also remind yourself that ultimately, you get to choose what your relationship with that person looks like. What we can't control is the other person. Don't expect the other person to change; instead, focus on how you respond to the person.

Prioritizing Social Well-Being

The quality of our relationships has a profound impact on our health and happiness. By prioritizing and nurturing meaningful connections, we can enhance our emotional resilience and capacity for personal growth and healing. Remember, building and maintaining relationships requires effort and intention, but the rewards are immense. Surround yourself with positive influences, practice empathy and compassion, and don't hesitate to release relationships that no longer serve you. Your social well-being is an integral aspect of your healing journey, deserving of attention and care.

By embracing the power of relationships, you take a significant step towards a healthier, happier, and more fulfilling life. This does take focus and intention to create a habit of finding friends. To begin with, in your morning journaling practice, write a loving message to yourself each day to strengthen that most important relationship: your relationship with yourself. Also, be deliberate about fostering external relationships with a daily practice of connecting with at least one person each day. This could be as simple as sending a message or calling, or it could be planning a get-together with a friend or group of friends. Pay close attention to how you feel when you are with certain people. If you notice negative feelings, you may need to revisit Healing Habit #6, Forgive and Release. You may need to take a break or remove yourself from that relationship, even temporarily.

Summary of Healing Habit #9: Find Your Friends

- Set aside a few minutes in your morning for a daily journaling practice.
- Each morning, complete this sentence in your journal: "Today's loving message to myself is …"
- Every morning, complete this sentence in your journal: "A person I could connect with today by calling, or sending a message, or showing appreciation is …" and follow through on that intention.
- Honestly assess the relationships in your life. If there are relationships that cause you stress, forgive and release the people involved with compassion (Healing Habit #6) and plan a strategy for lessening or ending contact with the person or people.

You've established a strong morning practice by now with many of your Healing Habits. Now you'll add in morning journaling. Your trigger for this new habit will be your other morning habits. Simply add another few minutes to write yourself a loving message and decide who you will connect with that day. During your weekly Forgive and Release habit, you could evaluate relationships in your life and decide if it's time to release relationships that are adding stress to your life. Make sure you add Find Your Friends to your morning practices in your Daily Habit Checklist and reward yourself with a checkmark each time you practice.

Healing Habit #10: Move with Joy

The human body is meant to move. As a cornerstone of overall health, movement impacts various bodily systems and contributes to physical, mental, and emotional well-being. Movement oxygenates cells, stimulates the lymphatic system, and strengthens the muscular-skeletal and cardiovascular system.

While we know movement is good for us, fear of movement is common for people with chronic pain. Although it might seem counterintuitive, research underscores the remarkable benefits that can be reaped through exercise to lower pain and improve overall health. Movement increases blood flow to affected areas, promoting healing and reducing inflammation. It also releases endorphins, the body's natural painkillers, which can help alleviate pain, improve mood, and increase energy.

Feeling Confident About Moving

It's important that you feel relaxed when engaging in any movement. If you've experienced fear of movement, then this may require a gradual approach to rebuild confidence in the body's ability to move without injury or pain. Starting with gentle movement, doing activities that you love will help relax the nervous system.

First, to reduce fear and anxiety associated with physical movement and to relax the nervous system, reassure your mind that it's safe to move your body. Start with small movements and a gentle approach, gradually increasing in intensity over time. It's okay if there is mild discomfort. Simply remind your mind that you are safe.

I love to dance! When I was in a lot of pain from rheumatoid arthritis, I was unable to dance like I used to. Instead, I would put on some of my favorite dance music and "chair dance" by grooving to the music while sitting down. I had a lot of fun with this, and that is what I focused on, rather than what I couldn't do. I could feel my mood elevating, and I could even get my heart rate up a little, too. Gradually, I could stand on my feet and dance and, eventually, could dance around the room again.

Movement for Mindfulness and Relaxation

Incorporating mindfulness and relaxation techniques into movement can help the nervous system relax. Practices like deep breathing and present-moment awareness during movement can help reduce stress and tension. These techniques promote relaxation and help in managing the emotional aspects of your health condition. Yoga, qigong, and Tai Chi incorporate relaxation into the movement, but you can include mindfulness and relaxation in just about any form of movement. Paying attention to the sensory experience of the movement is a great way to stay in the present moment and feel more relaxed. For example, if you're walking outdoors, you may notice the colors you see, the sounds you hear, the wind on your face, and the smells in the air.

The Power of Visualization

Visualization is a powerful tool that can be used alongside movement to enhance its benefits. When you visualize yourself moving with ease and joy, you create a mental blueprint that can influence your physical reality. This practice can help reduce fear and anxiety about movement and reinforce positive outcomes. Before engaging in physical activity, take a few moments to close your eyes and visualize yourself moving effortlessly and pain-free. Imagine the joy and freedom that comes with this movement, and let these positive feelings guide your actual experience.

The Joy of Movement

Feeling joy during movement is equally important as the physical benefits it provides. Exercise should not be viewed as a chore but as an opportunity to engage in activities that bring happiness and fulfillment. American choreographer and dancer, Martha Graham, observed, "All that is important is this one moment in movement. Make the moment important, vital, and worth living. Do not let it slip away unnoticed and unused." In other words, mindfully engage in the moment as you are moving, and feel joy in the moment.

Joyful movement can range from dancing and playing sports to hiking and practicing yoga. When we enjoy physical activity, we are more likely to stick with it, making it a sustainable part of our lifestyle.

Joyful movement also has profound mental and emotional benefits. It reduces stress, anxiety, and depression by promoting the release of endorphins and other mood-enhancing chemicals. It provides a sense of accomplishment and boosts self-esteem, contributing to a positive self-image.

Engaging in social physical activities, such as group sports or fitness classes, fosters a sense of community and connection with others. This social interaction is vital for mental well-being and can provide additional motivation to stay active.

Movement is not only a physical activity but also a form of self-expression. Dance, for instance, allows you to express your emotions and creativity. It provides a medium to connect with yourself on a deeper level, to explore your inner world, and to release pent-up emotions. This emotional release can be incredibly therapeutic, helping to alleviate the emotional components of living with a chronic condition.

Creating a Routine That Works for You

Creating a movement routine that works for you is essential for consistency and long-term benefits. Start by choosing activities that you genuinely enjoy and that fit into your daily schedule. Whether it's a morning yoga session, an afternoon walk, or a dance party in your living room, find what works best for you and make it a non-negotiable part of your day.

Engage in any form of physical movement that you find enjoyable. This can also help distract from pain or attention to physical symptoms. Any form of exercise that brings you pleasure can be beneficial. Remember, the goal is to move with joy, not to push yourself to the point of exhaustion or pain. Listen to your body and adjust the intensity and duration of your activities as needed. Celebrate small victories and progress, no matter how minor they may seem.

Summary of Healing Habit #10: Move with Joy

- Choose one activity that you enjoy doing or used to enjoy doing. Schedule a time to do this movement every day. Morning is a great time.
- Start small. Pay attention to your thoughts as you engage in the movement. If you are experiencing fear or you notice muscles bracing or tensing, remind your mind that you are safe, and feel your body relax. If you are still tense, then scale back a bit until you can feel your body relax.
- Practice being in the moment, using as many senses as possible, or simply notice your breath.
- Feel joy and appreciation for your body for helping you move.

This habit is a new daily commitment. Morning movement can contribute to better sleep at night, but you decide when the best time of day is for you. If you do decide to make Move with Joy part of your morning routine, then your morning habits can be the cue for this new habit. If you choose another time of day, decide what will "cue" this habit for you and set yourself up for success. To make this habit attractive, be aware of the positive feelings in your body as you move.

To make it easy, have whatever you need to incorporate daily movement ready to go. To make it satisfying, reward your brain by checking off on the Healing Habit Tracker every time you practice Move with Joy, or use your own tracking system.

Milestones for Step 5: Generate

- Healing Habit #9: Practice Find Your Friends daily and release non-supportive relationships.
- Healing Habit #10: Move with Joy every day with daily mindful movement.

Decide whether you want to integrate these habits at the same time or start with Healing Habit #9 until it becomes automatic, then add in Healing Habit #10.

The Generate step is complete when you have incorporated each of these habits with consistency until each becomes automatic for you, or for at least 28 days. Once these habits are automatic for you and you are practicing them most of the time, make sure you celebrate achieving these milestones. Look how far you've come, my friend! I'm celebrating you!

Now you're ready to move on to the last step in the DESIGN Blueprint, Navigate.

Chapter 10

Step 6: Navigate

"Do silly things. Foolishness is a great deal more vital and healthy than our straining and striving after a meaningful life."
—Anton Chekhov

You're on the last step of the DESIGN Blueprint: Navigate. This step is about being playful and curious, aligning with the flow of life and welcoming new experiences that expand your horizons and nurture your soul.

The two Healing Habits for Navigate are:

- Healing Habit #11: Play and Create
- Healing Habit #12: Learn, Grow, and Expand.

Let's learn about these two habits as we navigate through this last step and how they can help your body release pain.

Healing Habit #11: Play and Create

If you've been living with chronic pain, finding joy and expressing oneself creatively can seem like a pointless luxury rather than a necessity. You may feel like you're in too much pain to play or create anything. However, in this chapter, you're invited to rediscover the joy of play and the power of creativity as essential elements of healing. By recognizing that life is meant to be fun and exploring activities that bring joy, you tap into healing emotions that signal safety to your nervous system.

Engaging in playful activities and creative pursuits isn't just about having fun, it's about activating profound healing processes within your body and mind. Research has shown that playfulness and creativity can significantly reduce stress, enhance mood, and improve overall health.

For instance, studies have found that engaging in creative activities can lower cortisol levels, a key indicator of stress, and increase the production of endorphins, which promote a sense of well-being and happiness.

Also, creative expression has been linked to improved cognitive function and emotional resilience. Activities like painting, dancing, writing, or even gardening can stimulate the brain, enhance problem-solving skills, and promote emotional regulation. This holistic approach to health aligns perfectly with the concept of signaling safety to your nervous system, creating a fertile ground for healing. Along with these health benefits, many playful and creative activities can be done with others, fostering social connections and a sense of community. This social aspect is crucial for overall well-being and can provide additional emotional support.

I remember talking with my naturopath one day, when my healing seemed to be stuck. She surprised me with this question: "What are you doing for fun?" At first, I was taken aback because up to this point, our focus had been on supplements, diet, and so on. Her question made me realize I had been putting off having fun, thinking that I needed to heal first. Now, I know that fun and playfulness are part of the healing process. I see this in many of my students, too. They are so focused on their healing that they forget to enjoy life. When we are hyper-focused on healing, we can actually hinder our healing because the nervous system doesn't feel safe.

Incorporating Play and Creativity

Take some time to reflect on activities that bring you genuine joy. This isn't about proficiency or skill but about what makes you feel alive and happy. Think back to things you enjoyed as a child and current interests to identify activities that resonate with your authentic self. Make a list of these activities that ignite your passion and spark joy.

Set aside dedicated time each week for one or more of your chosen activities. Even small, regular intervals can make a significant difference in your well-being. When engaging in creative pursuits, focus on the process rather than the outcome. Allow yourself the freedom to express and enjoy without judgment. This mindset shift is essential for reaping the full benefits of play and creativity.

After my conversation with my naturopath, I thought, *What do I want to do for fun?* I had never taken an art class, so I decided to sign up for a drawing and watercolor course. I found the act of creating and focusing a beautiful distraction. I didn't think about my health at all while I was painting. Over time, I noticed a significant reduction in my stress levels and an improvement in my overall mood. Now, I paint just for the pure joy of it, and I let go of judgments about my work.

Dr. Stuart Brown, a pioneer in the study of play, emphasizes, "Play is not a luxury. Play is a necessity." His research highlights the critical role of play in maintaining emotional and physical health.

Overcoming Obstacles to Play

Common barriers such as time constraints, self-doubt, lack of resources, or physical limitations can hinder your ability to incorporate play as a modality of healing. If any of these are holding you back, let's address them now.

- **Time Constraints:** If you feel limited by time, start with small, manageable chunks. Even 10 minutes a day dedicated to a creative activity can make a difference. You can gradually increase the time as you become more comfortable and see (and feel!) the benefits.
- **Self-Doubt:** Focus on the enjoyment of the activity rather than the outcome. The goal is to have fun and express yourself. Give yourself permission to create or play without judgment, and celebrate the process rather than the end result.

- **Lack of Resources:** Many creative activities require minimal resources. For example, writing, drawing, and dancing can be done with just a pen and paper or your own body. Explore online resources and communities that offer free tutorials and inspiration for creative activities.
- **Pain or Movement Limitations:** Adapt activities to suit your physical abilities. For instance, if you have limited mobility, you might engage in seated or lying-down forms of creative expression, such as drawing, knitting, or digital art. Gentle movement activities like Tai Chi or chair yoga can also be beneficial. Consult with a healthcare provider to find activities that are safe and enjoyable for you.

Incorporating play and creativity into your life isn't just a pleasant addition; it's a vital component of your healing journey. By engaging in activities that bring joy and allow for creative expression, you signal safety to your nervous system, reduce stress, and enhance your overall well-being. Embrace the freedom to play and create, and invite your soul to shine through these joyful pursuits. Remember, life is meant to be enjoyed, and by prioritizing play and creativity, you open the door to a more vibrant, healthy, and fulfilling life.

Summary of Healing Habit #11: Play and Create

- Make a list of activities or interests that you enjoy, that you used to enjoy, or that you would like to do.
- Choose one activity on the list and identify the next steps you need to take to make it happen.
- Schedule a time in the next week to take the next steps or do the activity.
- Do the thing! Embrace the process rather than the outcome, enjoying the freedom to express without judgment.

To bring Healing Habit #11 to life, first, set aside time in your weekly review to make that list of activities or interests, and then pick one to be your next goal. Identify what your next steps are to bring that into your life and schedule when you will take those steps. Make this habit satisfying by celebrating your Play and Create success.

Healing Habit #12: Learn, Grow, and Expand

Human beings are naturally inclined towards growth and expansion. This intrinsic desire is a fundamental aspect of our existence, and I believe it comes from our soul. Empowerment leader, Anthony J. D'Angelo, has said, "Develop a passion for learning. If you do, you will never cease to grow." For individuals with chronic pain, embracing the desire for lifelong learning becomes an essential component of the healing journey. By recognizing that growth is inherent to human nature and embracing learning as a lifelong pursuit, you can tap into your innate desire for personal evolution and self-discovery.

Lifelong Learning Is Good for Your Health

Scientific research strongly supports the connection between lifelong learning and improved health. For those with chronic pain, this can be particularly beneficial as it helps to alleviate stress, improve mood, and enhance overall well-being.

Lifelong learning promotes neuroplasticity, enabling the brain to reorganize itself by forming new neural connections throughout life—a skill that lends itself to retraining the brain to release pain. Additionally, continuous learning is associated with improved mental health and well-being, reducing symptoms of depression and anxiety while enhancing self-esteem and providing a sense of purpose and achievement. The social engagement often involved in learning, whether through formal education, community courses, or informal groups, has been linked to lower risks of mortality and cognitive decline, indicating significant benefits for overall health and longevity. Engaging in learning activities can also reduce stress levels by providing enjoyable and stimulating distractions from everyday worries, thereby lowering cortisol levels and promoting relaxation. Furthermore, lifelong learning has been shown to improve cognitive functions like memory, attention, and problem-solving skills, which are crucial for enhancing quality of life, especially in older adults.

Overall, the scientific evidence highlights the profound impact of lifelong learning on both mental and physical health, underscoring its importance for those with chronic pain seeking to enhance their well-being and embark on a fulfilling journey of self-discovery and healing.

From a spiritual standpoint, learning and growth are vital for awakening the intrinsic learner within each of us. Spiritual traditions across cultures emphasize the importance of knowledge and wisdom in achieving higher states of consciousness and inner peace. Engaging in activities that expand our understanding of the world and ourselves can lead to profound spiritual and personal growth, fostering a deeper connection with our true selves and the universe.

Rekindling Your Desire for Learning

While living with chronic pain, you may have neglected (like I did) your desire for learning, which is completely understandable. Focusing your attention on growth and expansion rather than your limitations will help you heal. Your brain will naturally create new neural networks based on your desire for learning new things. When you make time for learning, you are sending a message to your brain and nervous system that you are safe, helping your body release the need for protection in the form of pain.

Incorporating learning into daily life requires consistency and intentionality. To do this, you will make learning a regular part of your daily routine. By scheduling time for activities such as reading, watching documentaries, listening to podcasts, or taking courses, you will commit to nurturing your intellectual curiosity and expanding your horizons.

Embracing Limitless Possibilities

Growth often requires stepping out of our comfort zones and embracing new challenges. By adopting a mindset of continuous learning and growth, you will open yourself up to new experiences and opportunities. What if you had the time and resources to learn about anything? What would you want to learn about? Have you always been interested in astronomy, Mozart, or Greek mythology, for example? Make a list of topics you wish to explore further and outline actionable steps to pursue learning opportunities. In this way, you can begin to take action toward your personal growth and expansion.

As you commit to embracing a mindset of continuous learning and growth, you'll unlock the potential within you to evolve and thrive, empowering you to live fully in the present moment, seizing opportunities for growth and learning as they arise, rather than putting off your interests. By embracing your curiosity and desire for learning, you'll also support your body's ability to heal, both of which can be the catalyst to transform your life.

Learning and growth are more fulfilling when shared with others. For that reason, finding like-minded people can help with support and encouragement on your learning journey. Whether through study groups, online communities, or local clubs, connecting with others who share similar interests can enhance the learning experience and provide valuable support.

Personalizing Your Journey of Learning and Growth

The journey of learning and growth is a vital part of your healing path. By nurturing your intellectual curiosity, embracing new experiences, and finding supportive communities, you can significantly enhance your well-being and embark on a fulfilling journey of self-discovery and healing.

You may not have given much thought to what you would like to learn more about, so begin by making a list of twenty or more topics you're interested in. For inspiration, you could reflect on things that interested you as a child. Study the list and decide which topic you would like to delve into first. Brainstorm on ideas for how you could learn more. Are there books, podcasts, or groups on the topic? Could you take a course to learn more about this topic? Think about how you could incorporate learning a little about this topic every day, even if it's just a few minutes. Schedule time to do this every day.

You probably know by now how much I love using the mornings to accomplish goals! Part of my morning routine is to read for at least ten minutes. I do this after all the other morning habits we've talked about thus far. Ten minutes may not seem like much, but it adds up. Even if I only read ten minutes a day, on average, that is about one book every two months. I like to listen to podcasts while I'm driving, walking, or doing housework. We can all find at least ten minutes in our day to dedicate to learning.

Summary of Healing Habit #12: Learn, Grow, and Expand

- Make a list of twenty or more topics you would like to learn more about.
- Choose one topic to begin exploring more deeply.
- Select your learning medium, such as a book, a podcast, joining a group, or taking a course.
- Schedule a time every day for reading and learning, even if it's as little as ten minutes.

You could incorporate daily learning as part of your morning routine, midday rest time, or part of your wind-down routine at night. Decide when you'll do it, and what will be the cue for this habit. Add it to your Healing Habit Tracker and make it satisfying by checking off each time you Learn, Grow, and Expand.

Milestones for Step 6: Navigate

- Healing Habit #11: Incorporate Play and Create time at least once a week.
- Healing Habit #12: Learn, Grow, and Expand daily in an area that interests you.

Decide whether you want to integrate these habits at the same time or start with Healing Habit #11 until it becomes automatic, then add in Healing Habit #12, whatever works best for you.

The Integrate step is complete when you have incorporated each of these habits with consistency until each becomes automatic for you, or for at least 28 days. Once these habits are automatic and you are practicing them most of the time, celebrate your achievement. You've now implemented all twelve of the Healing Habits! Congratulations, my friend!

PART III:
Life by DESIGN

Chapter 11

Living Your Life by DESIGN

"Lead a life of your own design, on your own terms. Not one that others or the environment have scripted for you."
—Tony Robbins

Most people drift through life, reacting to circumstances, following routines they never consciously chose, and wondering why they feel stuck. But healing, growth, and true transformation don't happen by accident; they happen by design. When you live life on purpose, you become the engineer of your own experience. You step out of reaction mode and into creation mode. Instead of being at the mercy of old patterns, you consciously shape your days, your habits, and ultimately, your future. Living pain-free, living fully, requires making a choice: Will you let life happen to you, or will you design a life that aligns with your highest vision?

I hope that by now, you're experiencing the results of living life by DESIGN. I hope that you're feeling less pain as your nervous system shifts to the relaxation response, more and more often. Becoming pain-free on purpose isn't about luck or willpower; it's about creating a life that naturally supports your healing. And that happens through consistent, intentional action. Change doesn't come from wishing or waiting; it comes from daily choices that align with the vision of the life you want to live. To make this process simple and sustainable, I've developed a four-step weekly system, a structured yet flexible framework to help you reflect, plan, schedule, and take action. This system isn't about perfection; it's about progress. It will help you stay accountable, build momentum, and make your healing habits second nature, so that living pain-free becomes not just possible, but inevitable. Let's go through this system.

The Weekly System

The four-step weekly system is a simple guideline to help you be successful on the DESIGN Blueprint. The four steps of this system are: Reflect, Plan, Schedule, and Execute. When you reflect on your journey and celebrate your progress, plan for success, schedule what matters, and take inspired action, you are consciously building a life that supports healing, energy, and ease. As we go through this system, please refer to the following three resources *Weekly Review & Preview Worksheet, Weekly Planning Sheet,* and *Daily Pages.* You can find these in the Resources section of this book and also download them by going to http://painfreeonpurpose.com/ or scanning the QR Code on page 158.

1. Reflect: Look Back to Move Forward

Each week begins with reflection, an opportunity to pause, take stock of your journey, and gather insights from your experiences. Reflection is not about dwelling on mistakes; rather, it's about learning, growing, course-correcting with kindness, and celebrating what went well.

Use the Weekly Review area of the *Weekly Review & Preview Worksheet* to reflect on:

- Your three biggest wins from last week: What went well? Why was it meaningful?
- The progress you made on your top goals from the previous week: Celebrate your wins. Even small steps matter.
- Challenges and lessons learned: Every challenge carries wisdom.
- Your thoughts, emotions, and actions: How did you show up for yourself?
- Anyone you need to forgive or release judgment toward: Application of Healing Habit #8.

This process keeps you conscious and intentional, helping you reinforce what works and adjust what doesn't.

2. Plan: Set Your Intentions for the Week

Once you've reflected and celebrated, it's time to plan for the week ahead. This step turns your healing intentions into an actionable plan, ensuring that your priorities don't get lost in the busyness of life.

Use the Weekly Preview area of the *Weekly Review & Preview Worksheet* to:

- Set three big goals for the week: What matters most right now?
- Decide how you will nourish your body: What foods, movement, or self-care will support you?
- Plan for fun and creativity: Healing isn't just about discipline; joy is essential.
- Choose something to learn and explore: Growth keeps you inspired.

Planning ensures that you show up for yourself in a meaningful way, week after week.

3. Schedule: Turn Your Plan Into Reality

Now it's time to put your plans into your schedule. What gets scheduled gets done, not because of force, but because of clarity.

Use the Weekly Planning Sheet to:

- Block out time for your top three goals.
- Schedule commitments, appointments, and priorities.
- Organize your healing habits: morning, midday, and evening routines.

When you schedule with intention, you create more space for spontaneity, ease, and alignment.

4. Execute: Take Inspired Action

The final step is living out your plan, not perfectly, but consistently. Taking small, intentional actions each day leads to lasting transformation.

Each morning, use the left side of the *Daily Pages* to:

- Set your top three goals for the day.
- Track your morning healing habits.
- Set your Morning Mindset up for anticipation and connection.
- Write a loving message to yourself.

Use the middle section of the *Daily Pages* to schedule your activities and commitments, transferring items from the *Weekly Planning Sheet*. Use the bottom of the middle section to track how much water you drink throughout the day. A general guideline is to drink half your body weight in pounds as ounces. For example, a person weighing 200 lbs would need to drink 100 oz of water, or about twelve 8-oz glasses of water. If you are drinking much less than the guideline, build up to that amount over time.

Use the right side of the *Daily Pages* to:

- Track your midday and evening healing habits.
- Do an Evening Reflection to:
    - Celebrate what you did well.
    - Acknowledge any challenges with kindness.
    - Reflect on that day's thoughts and feelings.
    - Identify your biggest win of the day, even if it was simply a new awareness.

By following these steps, you'll easily live a Healing Habit lifestyle. Healing happens in the small, consistent daily actions. When you reflect, plan, schedule, and take action, you are not just moving toward a pain-free life; you are actively creating it.

Your Next Evolution: Revisiting the DESIGN Blueprint

Healing is a continuous unfolding rather than a destination, and growth is a lifelong journey. And now that you've walked this path, it's time to dream even bigger. You have already used the DESIGN Blueprint to transform your life. You've gained clarity, built healing habits, and cultivated resilience. But transformation doesn't stop here.

Now, you are in a new place. You are stronger, wiser, and more in tune with your body than ever before. You've gained a new awareness, and new possibilities are opening up for you. Once you've achieved your original vision, it's time to revisit the DESIGN Blueprint with a fresh vision.

How to Evolve with the DESIGN Blueprint

- **Desire:** What does the next level of your healing look like? What new vision excites and inspires you? Maybe it's deeper emotional healing, a new adventure, or a commitment to even greater vitality. Dare to dream beyond what once felt possible.
- **Explore:** What messages are you getting from your intuition and your body to help you reachyour new vision? Are there healing modalities you're curious about? Keep expanding your understanding of what's possible.
- **Surrender:** What limiting beliefs or old stories no longer serve this new version of you? What can you release to step into this new phase with trust and openness? Can you surrender to the process and trust the outcome?
- **Integrate:** How can you bring this next vision into your daily life by nourishing your body and living more naturally? What foods, routines, mindsets, and rituals will anchor this transformation and support your physical transformation? Small, consistent actions create lasting change.

- **Generate:** Who are you becoming? What energy are you stepping into and emitting? Who are you surrounding yourself with? You are no longer just someone seeking healing, you are someone living and embodying it and generating supportive energy.
- **Navigate:** Life will continue to change, and so will you. How will you navigate challenges with grace? How will you stay open, adaptable, and in tune with your inner wisdom? Listen to guidance from your soul to find more joy and expand your experiences in this life with a new vision of what's possible for you.

Your Evolution Is a Gift

This next version of your journey is an opportunity, an invitation to step into even greater alignment, joy, and freedom.

So, take a deep breath, place your hand on your heart, and ask yourself: *What's next?*

Let the answer rise. Let it inspire and delight you. And then, as you have done before, take the first step.

Because this is your life, designed by you, for you, you are the writer, producer, director, and actor in your life. You are meant to be the hero of your life's story.

You Are the Hero You've Been Seeking

If you've made it to this part of the book, you are already in the top 10% of people who take action. You've done more than just read; you've committed to transformation. That alone sets you apart. Because healing isn't about consuming information, it's about applying it, one step at a time.

And now, you stand at a pivotal moment. The truth is, you were never broken. You never needed someone else to "fix" you. The power was always within you, and pain was a calling to awaken you to a better version of you, the *real* you that you came here to be. Your body is wise. Your mind is adaptable and creative. Your spirit is unbreakable.

Now, you have the tools, the knowledge, and the systems to support your healing. But more importantly, you have something even greater: a deepened belief in yourself. So hold onto your vision. Keep taking steps, even when they feel small. Because small steps, taken consistently, create massive change.

When you achieve the vision you set for yourself today, dream even bigger.

Keep your life simple. Plan and schedule, not for rigidity, but for freedom. Let your structure support your expansion.

And above all, live your life with a heart full of heroism. Because you are not just healing, you are leading. You are setting an example. You are showing others that healing is possible, and that living pain-free is a choice within reach.

A Blessing for Your Journey

As you step forward into this new chapter of your life, may you feel strong, free, and empowered.

May you wake up each morning with a deep knowing that you have the power to create your day, your health, and your future.

May you trust the intelligence of your body, the resilience of your mind, and the infinite wisdom of your soul.

May you find joy in the process, courage in the challenges, and love in the moments in between.

May you continue to grow, expand, and inspire those around you, not by striving, but by simply being the radiant, powerful being that you are. You are creating a positive ripple effect, impacting everyone you touch.

And when doubt arises, as it inevitably will, may you remember this: You are the hero you've been waiting for. I can't wait to see what you do!

Stand in your power and live pain-free on purpose.

RESOURCES

SCAN THIS CODE
TO ACCESS ADDITIONAL BOOK RESOURCES

http://painfreeonpurpose.com

HEALING HABIT TRACKER

WEEK OF: _____

MY MOTIVATION:

MORNING ROUTINE	M	T	W	T	F	S	S
	○	○	○	○	○	○	○
	○	○	○	○	○	○	○
	○	○	○	○	○	○	○
	○	○	○	○	○	○	○
	○	○	○	○	○	○	○

MIDDAY ROUTINE							
	○	○	○	○	○	○	○
	○	○	○	○	○	○	○
	○	○	○	○	○	○	○
	○	○	○	○	○	○	○

EVENING ROUTINE							
	○	○	○	○	○	○	○
	○	○	○	○	○	○	○
	○	○	○	○	○	○	○
	○	○	○	○	○	○	○
	○	○	○	○	○	○	○

RATE MY WEEK: ☆ ☆ ☆ ☆ ☆

Weekly Review & Preview

Weekly Review
Three great things that happened for me last week and why they are important were ...
Last week, I made the following progress on my three biggest goals ...
My biggest challenge last week and what I learned from it was ...
Thinking about my thoughts, feelings, and actions, I would say this about last week ...
A person or people I need to forgive or judge less harshly and the best ways I can do this is/are ...
Weekly Preview
I can nourish my body in a better way this week by ...
A way I can embrace living in harmony with nature this week is ...
Something I can do for fun or creativity this week is ...
A topic I would like to learn more about and the way I will do that this week is ...
My three biggest goals for this week are ...
And now ... schedule these on the Weekly Planning Sheet!

Also available as a download from painfreeonpurpose.com

Weekly Planning Sheet

Weekly Planning	Monday ___/___	Tuesday ___/___	Wednesday ___/___	Thursday ___/___	Friday ___/___	Saturday ___/___	Sunday ___/___
Events							
Projects							
Tasks							
Meals							

Daily Pages

DATE: ____ / ____ / ____

My top 3 goals for today are:		Midday Habit Tracker
1	5	□ Visioning
2	6	□ Affirmations
3		□ Mindfulness
Morning Habit Tracker	7	□ Rest
□ Visioning		**Evening Habit Tracker**
□ Affirmations	8	□ Visioning
□ Mindfulness		□ Affirmations
□ Get Outdoors	9	□ Mindfulness
□ Movement		□ Wind Down Routine
Morning Mindset	10	**Evening Reflection**
Something I am looking forward to or excited about today is …	11	A situation or person I handled well today was …
	12	
A person/people I can connect with or appreciate today and how I will do that is …	1	I could have made today even better if I …
	2	
One word that describes the kind of person I want to be today and why I chose it is …	3	Today I managed my thoughts and feelings by …
	4	
	5	
Today's loving message to myself is …	6	The best thing that happened today was …
	7	
	8	
	9	
	Today's Hydration □□□□□□□□□□	

Also available as a download from painfreeonpurpose.com

REFERENCES

Ashar, Y. K., Gordon, A., Schubiner, H., et al. (2022). Effect of pain reprocessing therapy vs placebo and usual care for patients with chronic back Pain: a randomized clinical trial. *JAMA Psychiatry, 79*(1), 13–23. doi: 10.1001/jamapsychiatry.2021.2669. PMID: 34586357.

Beecher, H. K. (1955). The powerful placebo. *Journal of the American Medical Association, 159*(17), 1602–1606.

Calvin, W. No magic number for the time it takes to form habits. Caltech. (April 17, 2023).

Canfield, J. (2015). The success principles: How to get from where you are to where you want to be (10th anniversary edition). HarperCollins.

Cascio, C. N., O'Donnell, M. B., Tinney, F. J., Lieberman, M. D., Taylor, S. E., Strecher, V. J., Falk, E. B. (2016). Self-affirmation activates brain systems associated with self-related processing and reward and is reinforced by future orientation. *Soc Cogn Affect Neurosci,11*(4):621–9. doi: 10.1093/scan/nsv136. Epub 2015 Nov 5. PMID: 26541373; PMCID: PMC4814782.

Clear, J. (2018). Atomic habits: An easy and proven way to build good habits & break bad ones. Avery.

Cross, M. P., Acevedo, A. M., Leger, K. A., & Pressman, S. D. (2023). How and why could smiling influence physical health? A conceptual review. *Health psychology review, 17*(2), 321–343. https://doi.org/10.1080/17437199.2022.2052740

Fischetti, M., Christiansen, J. (2021). Our bodies replace billions of cells every day. *Scientific American magazine, Vol. 324, No. 4.* (April 2021), p. 76.

Gordon, A. Ziv, A. (2022). The way out: A revolutionary, scientifically proven approach to healing chronic pain. Avery.

Holt-Lunstad, J., Smith, T. B., Layton, J. B. (2010). Social relationships and mortality risk: A meta-analytic review. *PLoS Med., 7*(7):e1000316. doi: 10.1371/journal.pmed.1000316. PMID: 20668659; PMCID: PMC2910600.

Kabat-Zinn, J. (1990). Full catastrophe living: Using the wisdom of your body and mind to face stress, pain and illness. Random House.

Kreiman, G., Koch, C., Fried, I. (2000). Imagery neurons in the human brain. *Nature, 408*(6810):357–61. doi: 10.1038/35042575. PMID: 11099042.

Lally, P. et al. (2009). How habits are formed: Modelling habit formation in the real world. *European Journal of Social Psychology.* 16 July 2009. doi.org/10.1002/ejsp.674

Landeros, A. Does your body really 'reset' every 7 years? Here's the deal on cell regeneration. Medreport.foundation (Dec 2024).

Lipton, B. (2005). The biology of belief: Unleashing the power of consciousness, matter and miracles (10th ed). Hay House.

Maté, G. (2003). When the body says no: The hidden cost of stress. Vintage Canada.

Nerurkar, A., Bitton, A., Davis, R. B., Phillips, R. S., Yeh, G. (2013). When physicians counsel about stress: Results of a national study. *JAMA Intern Med., 173*(1):76–77. doi:10.1001/2013.jamainternmed.480

Pert, C. (1997). Molecules of emotion: The science behind mind-body medicine. Scribner.

Petruccelli, K., Davis, J., Berman, T. (2019). Adverse childhood experiences and associated health outcomes: A systematic review and meta-analysis. *Child Abuse Negl. 2019 Nov*; 97:104127. doi: 10.1016/j.chiabu.2019.104127. Epub 2019 Aug 24. PMID: 31454589.

Putnam, F.W. (1989). Diagnosis and treatment of multiple personality disorder. Guilford Press.

Ramachandran, V. S., & Hirstein, W. (1998). The perception of phantom limbs: The D. O. Hebb lecture. *Brain, 121*(9), 1603–1630.

Ranganathan, V. K., Siemionow, V., Liu, J. Z., Sahgal, V., Yue, G. H. (2004). From mental power to muscle power-gaining strength by using the mind. *Neuropsychologia, 42*(7):944–56. doi: 10.1016/j.neuropsychologia.2003.11.018. PMID: 14998709.

Schubiner, H. (2022). Unlearn your pain: A 28-day process to unlearn your pain (4th ed). Mind Body Publishing.

Shochet, B.R. et al. (1969). A medical-psychiatric study of patients with rheumatoid arthritis. *Psychosomatics 10, No. 5*, (September-October 1969), p. 274.

Umberson, D., Montez, J. K. (2010). Social relationships and health: A flashpoint for health policy. *J Health Soc Behav. 2010*;51 Suppl(Suppl):S54–66. doi: 10.1177/0022146510383501. PMID: 20943583; PMCID: PMC3150158.

Wartolowska, K., Judge, A., Hopewell, S., et al. (2014). Use of placebo controls in the evaluation of surgery: Systematic review. *BMJ*, 348, g3253.

ACKNOWLEDGEMENTS

This book is the result of many hands, hearts, and moments of grace.

First, I acknowledge my inner guidance and the higher power that spoke to me at my rock-bottom moment. That quiet wisdom whispered, *You can heal,* and from that spark, everything changed.

To my beloved husband, Noel, my rock and the wind beneath my wings, you are everything. To my children, Nick, Kelsey, and Riley, you are my heart, and you inspire me to be the best version of myself. To my "new" children, Kat, Adam, and Terri, thank you for bringing your love and energy into my life. And to Mr. Tibbs, my loyal feline companion, who's been curled beside me through every chapter, thank you for your quiet, steady presence, even if you did knock over a glass of water—or several.

To my mother, whose love has lasted beyond your lifetime, I can feel you watching over me just as you said you would. To my father and siblings, who gave me the lessons I needed to learn and whose love is never in doubt, I carry you with me always.

I am deeply grateful to the Institute for Functional Medicine and the Functional Medicine Coaching Academy for opening the door to a whole new career and showing me what's possible beyond the conventional path. And to Dr. Aimie Apigian, your inspiration, wisdom, and the beautiful foreword you wrote are deeply cherished.

To the hundreds of clients and students who have trusted me to be their guide—you are my greatest teachers. Your courage to believe in yourselves and your capacity for healing continue to move and inspire me.

To the publishing team at She Rises Studios, thank you for helping turn this vision into reality.

To Maureen, who first asked, "What if ...", thank you for giving me permission to dream. Rebecca, Sheri, and Veronica, you've journeyed every step of this journey with me. Your belief and friendship have carried me forward. To Heather, for encouraging me to Think Big, and to Mary Agnes, whose solid guidance helped me step beyond my comfort zone and into a world of possibilities, thank you for expanding my world. And to the many friends, mentors, and soul supporters, too numerous to name, who offered encouragement, wisdom, and kindness when I needed it most, please know I hold deep gratitude for you.

Lastly, to my former self, the version of me that doubted, that hurt, that wasn't sure she'd ever feel whole again, you are the seed from which this entire book grew. Your pain became purpose, and that purpose became a mission.

May this book serve as a reminder to every reader: healing is possible, and the hero you've been waiting for ... is you.

ABOUT THE AUTHOR

Jane Hogan, "The Wellness Engineer," blends proven leading-edge science and ancient spiritually-inspired practices to help people release chronic pain using the mind, body, and breath to become empowered creators of their health.

Her personal experience of reversing crippling rheumatoid arthritis using natural solutions inspired her to leave a 30-year engineering career and become a Functional Medicine Certified Health Coach, Certified Yoga Teacher, and wellness educator.

Jane is the host of the *Wellness by Design* podcast, and her empowering message has been featured on numerous podcasts and summits. Her writing has been published in *Thrive Global* and *Elephant Journal* magazines, and she is a contributing author for three best-selling books, including *1 Habit for Entrepreneurial Success, Heal Me,* and *When Life Gives You Lemons Make Coconut Milk.* In 2022, Jane hosted the

Becoming Pain-Free: Healing the Root Causes of Chronic Pain online summit, empowering over 36,000 participants.

Jane's mission is to reveal how pain can serve as a catalyst for profound personal transformation. She guides others to discover their innate healing abilities by connecting with the power of who they truly are as creators of their life experiences—a philosophy that underlies all of Jane's teachings.

The tiny hamlet of Steady Brook on the island of Newfoundland, Canada, is Jane's home with her husband of thirty-five years, Noel, and their Maine Coon rescue cat, Mr. Tibbs. Newfoundland's rugged landscape provides the perfect backdrop for Jane's favorite outdoor pursuits: hiking, camping, kayaking, paddle boarding, skiing, snowshoeing, and cold-water immersion. Jane and Noel love to travel and spend time with their three adventurous adult children, Nick, Kelsey, and Riley.

JOIN THE MOVEMENT!

#painfreeonpurpose

With The Wellness Engineer

Join us in creating a world where everyone reclaims their power to heal, lives in harmony with their body, mind, and spirit, and inspires others to do the same.
We want to ignite a global awakening that empowers people to overcome chronic pain and illness by integrating science-backed practices, spiritual insight, and community-driven support.

Helping people find freedom from chronic pain so they can live their best lives.

Join the community of like minded souls using proven science and ancient spiritual wisdom to heal from the inside out.

LEARN MORE

Is chronic pain impacting your quality of life?

There is so much you can do to help your body release pain, proven by leading-edge science.

Contact us to learn more:
support@thewellnessengineer.com

SEE WHAT WE DO

OUR PODCAST   **OUR COMMUNITY**   **OUR OFFERINGS**

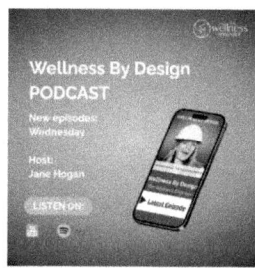 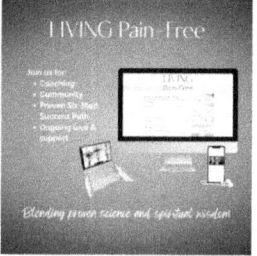 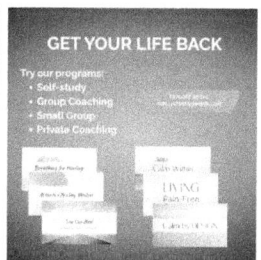

Learn from us!

Listen or watch the Wellness by Design podcast on YouTube, Apple Podcasts, Spotify or iHeart Radio.

Join our email community to receive our weekly *Friday Thrive* email with tools to help you!
https://thewellnessengineer.com/subscribe

Follow us on social media!

@janehoganhealth and @thewellnessengineer